ERIC TREACY'S
LMS

Frontispiece: This symbolic opening of the door to 'Eric Treacy's LMS' features rebuilt 'Royal Scot' No.46127 Old Contemptibles *at Holyhead shed being cleaned and made ready to work the 'up' 'Irish Mail' in 1948.*

ERIC TREACY's
L·M·S

David Jenkinson BSc, FRSA

&

Patrick Whitehouse ARPS

Oxford Publishing Co.

Cover and above: This powerful and typical Treacy picture shows Stanier 'Jubilee' No.5671 Prince Rupert *storming through Whitmore in 1937 with an 'up' express. Not untypically, Treacy does not identify the precise date or train; he was after a picture and he surely succeeded. The engine is, in fact, based at Edge Hill and the second carriage is ex-Lancashire & Yorkshire, so a Liverpool-London working seems a fairly safe bet.*

Title page:
Ex-LNWR 'Precursor' 4-4-0 No.25310 Thunderer *at Wavertree c1937 with a Liverpool to Holyhead express.*

A FOULIS-OPC Railway Book

This edition published 1988 by Guild Publishing by arrangement with the Haynes Publishing Group.

Publisher's note: Some of the more historic illustrations have been taken from glass plate negatives and it will be noticed that some slight deterioration, such as scratches and blemishes, have occurred during the intervening years.

Contents

Introduction

It is still with a sense of disbelief as I pen these lines, that I recall that fateful day in May 1978 when I bade farewell to Bishop Eric Treacy at Appleby, only to be told, 45 minutes later, as I stepped off *Evening Star* at Garsdale that he was with us no more. It scarcely sank in then and it still seems unreal now, for I felt that I had lost a lifelong friend even though I had known him personally for only eight short years. He was that sort of man and he was indeed my friend. That I should now be entrusted with compiling what is the first full length book wholly devoted to his pictures of but one railway simply adds to my disbelief. However, I like to think he would, perhaps, have done it himself had he lived longer and by way of introduction to what follows, I hope I may be forgiven for recounting some of the reasons why.

I first met Eric Treacy in person in 1970, during the course of my research for pictures of the Settle and Carlisle railway. Like most of my generation, I already felt I knew him for I had been brought up on a rich diet of his published pictures for nigh on 30 years previously. Yet it was with some diffidence that I knocked on his door at the Bishop's Lodge, Wakefield in response to his characteristic invitation to 'Come and look for yourself'. I had never met a real Bishop before and did not know what to expect but I need have had no fear. From the outset I was made to feel as though I had known him half my life and within half an hour, he had divested himself of his clerical jacket, having decided that the simplest way to sort out this vast treasury of pictures was to spread them all over the study floor. This was most certainly not what I had expected – crawling about across a mountain of railway pictures in company with a shirt-sleeved Bishop of Wakefield! However, when the inevitable pot of tea appeared at 'mid-session' it was equally clear that the domestic authorities were not the least surprised at the scene. Needless to say, I got more pictures than I could ever use and thus began a friendship which I treasure more than most in my lifetime.

During one of many subsequent sessions, in this case shortly after he had retired to Keswick, I recall making quite a few observations about the amount of interesting historical detail which could be seen in his pictures and he was obviously intrigued by the extent to which his pictures, merely by passage of time, had become valuable historical archives. He actually admitted that half the information I was getting excited about was unknown to him and before long, we found ourselves half plotting something along the lines of this book. This was, however, only a few months before his death and things came to nought. Since then, other friends of Eric's, eminent in the railway photographic field, have had opportunity to accompany several more selections of his

After steam had departed from the main line, although Treacy tackled the diesels and electrics, one somehow felt he was always happiest with steam. The preservation scene gave him less scope than the real steam railway had done but even so, he still had the knack of producing the definitive image. One has to look twice at this picture to realise that it is not a contemporary view of Class 5 4-6-0 No.5025 piloted by another of the same type but is, in fact, a departure from Keighley on the Worth Valley Railway. Although the leading Class 5, No.45212 carries 'private' insignia on its tender, No.5025 is decorated in probably the most accurate ever 'preserved' rendition of the 1935 LMS mixed traffic livery.

7

This panorama of Carlisle Upperby shed in early BR days is indicative of Treacy's regular re-visiting of favoured locations. The engines on view are a very characteristic LMS mixture, three LMS standards (two Fowler, one Stanier) and a pair of ex-LNWR 0-8-0s. He took pictures of this scene on many occasions and further examples are analysed in greater detail in Chapter 10.

Although not perhaps the most spectacular of Eric Treacy's pictures, this nice 1948 view of Class 4P Compound 4-4-0 No.41086 at Llandudno station is a good example of the sort of picture which, forty years later, has great historic value. The locomotive livery is of the short-lived LMS-BR transitional form (BR number in LMS style characters on a plain black engine), the station itself still has LMS furniture (nameboard, platform barrow etc) and the leading carriage is a pre-1929 LMS standard, much altered by panel replacement.

work and comment on his talent, so it did seem that perhaps all had been usefully said. Judge my surprise, therefore, when in 1985 I was approached by the new custodian of his negatives, Patrick Whitehouse, with the invitation to compile the narrative for another book of 'Treacy' pictures. There were, apparently, rather more of them than had been supposed.

In a sense, the Bishop himself was to blame, for he was forever telling us that he had 'scraped the barrel' and this had lulled everyone into believing that there really was little more to be found. He probably believed it, though most of the rest of us were not so sure(!), for he was a photographer first and foremost, always seeking after that elusive perfect picture and extremely critical of his own output. Furthermore, he never claimed to be a railway historian and, it has to be admitted, was not the best organiser of his own output. For example, it is rare to find an exact date on his pictures and it was not until his collection had at last been rationalised that it became clear that it was more than worthwhile to go back to the well again.

When I received Mr Whitehouse's invitation, I recall suggesting that we might try a different approach, based on my conversations with Eric Treacy in 1977, and tackle the problem in a deliberately restrictive and structured way if the pictures so allowed. Pat readily concurred and thus the idea for 'Eric Treacy's LMS' came into being. Up till now, most of Treacy's work has been presented 'across the board' as a pot-pourri of wonderful images drawn from his whole repertoire. In this compilation, we have deliberately imposed some fairly strict criteria, fully explained later and we hope it will prove acceptable. Speaking personally, I would also like to think that Eric himself would have approved, for when all is said and done, it is still his talent which is being celebrated. On this latter point, however, some final words need to be said.

Eric Treacy's style is often instantly recognisable – almost as if he had signed every picture individually – and this can lead to an

occasional feeling that one has seen a particular picture before. Sometimes this is true but more often than not there is some subtle difference between that which one actually sees and that which one *thought* one was seeing. Thus, although not all the pictures in this book are new, there are many more unknown ones than at first might seem the case and those which have been seen before are, for the most part, only available in books long out of print. But in truth, I fancy that most lovers of Eric Treacy's pictures will not mind seeing a few old favourites again and for those with an LMS bent, they might even prefer it this way rather than mixed up with other 'foreign' systems! In any case, old or new, there is never cause to be dissatisfied at the sheer quality and impact of Treacy's visual images; they speak for themselves.

I have also tried to use Treacy's LMS pictures to illustrate some of the more general ideas which he pioneered, as well as to demonstrate the way in which his brilliant technique can come to the aid of an historian. Thus, where I have used old favourites I have often deliberately tried to present them in the context of railway history rather than pure railway pictorialism, often by no more than the simple expedient of publishing the image much larger than ever before or merely by using the whole negative rather than the part most well known. I hope that what they may thus lose in compositional perfection is more than compensated

This, of course, is the classic Treacy approach – a favoured locomotive type at a favoured location, in this case Wavertree. However, and perhaps because of his persistent returning to the same location, possibly to get the perfect picture, he often managed to record events of historic interest too, such as on this occasion where he captured something of a rarity at that time (c1937/8) – the pioneer blue streamliner No.6220 Coronation *on a day when it was* not *working the 'Coronation Scot'. The value of this repetition of visiting is further examined later in the book.*

10

This sort of view, dare I say it, almost became a Treacy 'cliché' down the years but when it first appeared, it probably seemed very 'avant garde'. Let's face it, a picture in which one cannot see the train, the tender type cannot be distinguished and precise details of the engine livery are almost totally obscured, was not quite what most photographers were doing in the mid-1930s! But as an evocation of the LMS in the 1930s, it could hardly be bettered. For the record, the engine is 'Royal Scot' No.6112 Sherwood Forester approaching Wavertree.

by the extra information they reveal.

So, here is just a small part of Eric Treacy's record of the London Midland & Scottish Railway as he saw it. It was the view of an artist rather than a historian and by no means comprehensively or systematically gained. It has given me immense pleasure to prepare it and I can only hope that the somewhat more systematic presentation of the material will enhance rather than impede the sheer pleasure of looking at it.

David Jenkinson
Knaresborough
1988

Unmistakably Treacy and unmistakably LMS, this first view, at Penrith c1937, shows the sort of approach by which he first drew attention to himself. It is not just a picture of an express getting under way, it is pure 'railway'. The main subject is 'Royal Scot' 4-6-0 No.6135 The East Lancashire Regiment *departing south. Treacy has chosen a steep angle which makes it hard to distinguish too much of the train but by so doing, and by getting just the right location, he has also managed to give us massive amounts of extra detail. On the left, a pair of ex-LNWR 0-6-0 goods engines simmering gently at the shed remind us that these veterans, nicknamed "Cauliflowers", were* still responsible for much of the work on the Keswick branch, while to the right, the water column and signals give the essential 'LNWR' background to the scene. The early LMS standard 0-6-0 on the extreme right, basically an ex-Midland design, not only prevents attention wandering out of the picture but acts as a 'time link' between the very old LNWR engines and the ultra modern 'Scot' and also emphasises the 'LMS' nature of the view. The workmen and the locomotive driver add the finishing human touch. Technically, it is nothing like the best ever Treacy view but as an encapsulation of the LMS Railway it is hard to beat.

Chapter 1

Treacy and the LMS

Although Eric Treacy never admitted to a favourite railway, there were, in fact, only ever two of the British 'Big Four' which received anything like comprehensive coverage from his camera, the LMS and the LNER. Of these two, only the LMS was to be favoured by much of his pre-BR activity for above all, Treacy was a busy clergyman whose opportunities for photography were very much fitted in around his pastoral activities – and these always took priority. He therefore never strayed very far from his current home base at any one point in time, save for the occasional holiday or visit elsewhere, so it is not too surprising that most of his output very much reflected the railway scene in the areas close to where he currently lived. Thus it was that the years from 1935 to Nationalisation were dominated first by his duties as a parish priest on Merseyside and, later as Rector of Keighley in the West Riding of Yorkshire. In the former case the railway territory was almost exclusively LMS and in the latter instance the LMS was probably the more significant part. Of course, his travels took him to other places too, but there was always a strong northern bias to his locations, presumably because these areas were at least attainable within the limited amount of spare time available.

In consequence, one finds him returning again and again to the same places, a fact which may unwittingly have helped to create the occasional sense of 'deja vu' in the end product already remarked in the introduction. However, the mere fact that Treacy, through circumstances dictated by his vocation, found himself going back to his favourite haunts time after time, has left us with an unparalleled record of changes, albeit within only a modest number of specific areas. The fact that his various moves within the Church heirarchy kept him in the north allowed him to return to locations which he had made peculiarly his own in earlier days. This sort of record of change is meat and drink to the latter day historian, in some ways far more useful than a more 'catholic' choice of locations would have been. Similarly, Treacy's obvious preference for certain types of subject, which in other photographers would have betokened monotony, seemed somehow in his case to add to the challenge and interest. Thus 'Eric Treacy's LMS' is by no means comprehensive in terms of its geography or even subject matter, but where it exists at all, it is most characterised by its infinite variations upon a few themes. Although this aspect will not be the only one addressed in these pages, it must inevitably form a major part.

A second constraining factor, this time not of Treacy's making, is that occasioned by the title of this book with its emphasis on the LMS and not BR. A conscious decision was made from the outset that it would include no views which contained anything which

the LMS had neither inherited nor designed, although this has not gone quite so far as to exclude everything taken after 31st December 1947. This is deliberate for a number of reasons. Firstly, it makes the title more honest than if post-LMS designs were allowed to intrude but secondly, by extending the period beyond Nationalisation for a few years, it also allows coverage of that fascinating early BR period which Treacy recorded so well when, livery apart, nothing much had changed. There are, of course, some casualties arising from this approach, not least the fact that Treacy took many of his best 'LMS' area pictures after the BR dilution factor had set in, including most of his work in Scotland during the 1950s and later.

So much for the parameters, what of his overall approach? As far as can be determined, Treacy had no specific theme to his picture taking save that of capturing the visual essence of the railway, so the grouping of images in this survey is more a reflection of how he seemed to see the LMS rather than on any notes or intentions expressed by him as to its underlying logic. There are, however, a few regularly repeated themes which seem worth exploring; these form the basis of the chapters which follow. In them, I have tried to assign topic headings to reflect what seems to me to be the main theme of the picture but there is a degree of compromise and overlap in my assessment; some views

Many of Treacy's views in open country were quite spectacular pictures but this view of Stanier 4-6-2 No. 6201 Princess Elizabeth, *climbing southward between Carlisle and Shap summit, c1937/8, is principally a superb record of a massive train. Not only can we pick out details of the engine itself, but because of the angle of view chosen, almost every single item in this 18 vehicle cavalcade can be positively identified if desired. The first three vehicles are seen to be, in order; LMS utility van, ex-WCJS six-wheel fish/milk van and an ex-LNWR full brake. There then follow 15 passenger carriages of which the first six (composed of examples from all three LMS design periods) form a self contained group with a brake at each end. Behind this is a dining 'pair', including one twelve-wheeler with kitchen, then an odd Stanier coach. The last six vehicles, all Stanier, form another self contained group including a second twelve-wheel kitchen/diner. It was probably 'The Mid-Day Scot' with separate Edinburgh and Glasgow sections.*

Treacy's close-up views can be examined at different levels. This clear picture, again taken c1937/8 shows an un-named and Preston based 'Patriot' class 4-6-0 No.5544 leaving its home town in the northbound direction on the West Coast Main Line with an unidentified express. The depot allocation (10B) can be read off the smokebox and the date can be established by the clarity of the livery, quite obviously newly applied, which shows red shaded insignia of scroll/serif style. This style did not appear until July 1937 – QED! The unidentified train was probably not one of the more important workings – if so it would more probably have been 'Scot' or 'Princess' hauled at this time on this route. Furthermore, the carriages themselves, such as can be seen, are of LNWR origin and at least twenty years old. However, most significantly of all, one can read the inscription on the end: 'Inter-Corridor Set No.68'. The latter were small three and four coach sets, often incorporating older corridor stock and kept semi-permanently coupled and thus available for the more secondary workings. They were far better than even the newest non-corridors in terms of passenger/luggage space and in this case these could well have been going to some-where like Barrow. All told, there is quite a lot of information on what, at first, seems to be a very simple picture.

could well have been put in a different context to that which I have chosen. I can only crave forgiveness from the reader if I have not always got it quite right.

To set the scene, however, and especially for the benefit of those new to his work, this first selection scans the whole range of his activity. From them it will readily be appreciated that a Treacy picture can be viewed at a variety of levels. Thus a picture of an express train can often tell us much about signalling while a posed engine shot can frequently reveal much of interest in the background. This is the lasting historic value of his work and I hope this first selection will help readers to understand why.

This is the sort of picture where emotion takes over. It is one of Treacy's earliest attempts in 1937 to capture the romance of the streamliners and shows No.6221 Queen Elizabeth *hauling the 'Coronation Scot' at Kilburn. It was widely used at the time for publicity purposes, the back of the print actually claiming it for the LMS Advertising & Publicity Department! It has not been seen for many years.*

Eric Treacy was a great rider of engine footplates and took many fine pictures from this vantage point – most of which are very familiar. It was not, however, until I was preparing this selection that I discovered this particular example. It is taken from the footplate of Stanier 4-6-2 No.6240 City of Coventry *(formerly streamlined) at the end of the climb to Shap Summit from Tebay. Again it shows his sense of 'environment', for it is hard to imagine a better place at which to depict these magnificent engines. Note too that he has also included the workmen's platform at the Summit itself – see also page 177.*

When not taking moving trains, Treacy still
sought for atmosphere and this splendid
study at Edge Hill gives a real feeling of the
character of an LMS steam depot in the
later 1930s. The date is probably 1938 and
one cannot be certain that he did not have
this fine array of engines wheeled out
especially for his benefit. Edge Hill was an
LNWR depot but by this time, the former
company influence had been much reduced,
having been replaced by the new LMS
types. There is only one ex-LNWR engine
in sight and even that is an LMS rebuild,
large boilered 'Claughton' class 4-6-0
No.5946 Duke of Connaught, second from
right. It is well outnumbered by the
predominantly Stanier or Midland lineaments of the rest. For the record, these are,
left to right: Stanier 'Princess Royal' Class
7P 4-6-2 No.6201 Princess Elizabeth,
Stanier 'Jubilee' Class 5XP 4-6-0 No.5601
British Guiana, LMS Class 4F 0-6-0
No.4180, ex-MR Class 4F 0-6-0 No.3908,
LMS Class 4P Compound 4-4-0 No.1160,
LMS Class 3F 0-6-0T No.7404.

After the war, Treacy moved to Keighley and it was not long before his cameras were active on the Aire Valley route of the former Midland Railway from Leeds, Bradford and Skipton to Carlisle and Morecambe. This is a Skipton view of the 'down' 'Thames-Clyde Express' in 1947, a train which passed in front of his lens many hundreds of times and of which a more detailed study is given in Chapter 5. On this occasion it was hauled by the pioneer rebuilt 'Royal Scot' 4-6-0 No.6103 *Royal Scots Fusilier*, one of several famous members of the class based at Leeds (Holbeck). Rebuilt in 1943, the engine is seen here in the post-war LMS express livery of glossy black with maroon and straw lining.

Treacy stated the rebuilt 'Scots' to be his favourite LMS engines and, no doubt, this was the reason for taking this posed picture at Hellifield of No.6133 *The Green Howards*, again in 1946 livery. With the passage of time, however, this picture is of almost more interest by virtue of the subsidiary details visible on the extreme left. In close juxtaposition one can see an original Midland platform lantern and shunting signal, an early LMS standard goods brake and one of the distinctive LMS pattern 'Hawkseye' station nameboards, introduced in 1937. Such is the clarity of Treacy's picture that one can even differentiate between the background colour to the station name itself (yellow) and the main board (white).

This is yet another, apparently simple picture from which a whole host of information can be gained. The engine is a Stanier Class 5 4-6-0 No.5050, one of the original domeless 1934 built series; it now carries a dome. In addition to that, it has been repainted in the freight version of the 1946 LMS livery – ie unlined black with new style insignia. This was a somewhat rare treatment for plain black engines, save for new ones. As a general rule, only the express types were regularly repainted in the 1946 style at this time, but since Treacy probably obtained more records of this short-lived decorative phase than any other photographer, it is not surprising that he caught a few of the rarities.

The 11A shed plate visible on the original print reveals that the engine was based at Carnforth, thus suggesting that the train itself, although not identified by Treacy, was almost certainly a Morecambe bound semi-fast. This is supported by the carriage formation which, although at first sight quite random, is actually quite logical. It consists of two identical four coach portions formed up composite/third brake/third/full brake. It is a fair bet that one each came from Leeds and Bradford and were joined up at Shipley.

Within each formation, the full brakes are probably present in order to meet local operating needs (parcels?) and the centrally located brake within the remaining three-coach passenger carrying set was very common LMS practice where but one 'van' space was needed. By putting it in the middle, the set could operate in either direction when worked as a single unit, without offending against contemporary preference for not having too much train to the rear of the guard's compartment. It can be additionally noted that these two passenger carrying portions are, in fact, the opposite way round from each other. Modern BR practice is very different!

(Opposite). Treacy's 'landscape' railway views seemed to develop in scope and variety at about the time of transition from LMS to BR, maybe because it was now easier than it had been for him to get about – pre-war, for example, he is known to have cycled a good deal to get to his favourite places and this would impose severe limitations of choice. These two early BR scenes at Beattock exemplify this later phase. They are obviously railway, the trains are nothing special – typical late period LMS type 'Through Freights' (see Chapter 7) in charge of Class 5 4-6-0s – but the setting is what matters.

The uphill view of the banked freight was obviously taken from the valley floor in the upper right distance of the wider shot, probably at much the same time. Its purpose has nothing to do with the train details 'per se' but a great deal to do with the scale factor between train and environment. So too has the downhill view, for Treacy did not often photograph 'coasting' steam trains. In this case, the engine holds the foreground attention from which the eye moves into the distance as the line itself, obeying the dictates of the all too evident physical landscape, climbs to the distant watershed. One could conduct a geography lesson on these two pictures alone!

During the LMS/BR transition period, Treacy recorded many aspects of a scene which, by its very nature, was bound to be but transitory. It was, however, of great historical interest and no apology is offered for the many pictures of this period contained in these pages. This view, taken on one of his comparatively rare visits to Derby is typical. Everything about it is pure LMS, down to the delapidated train shed roof shortly to vanish. Paint the engines and carriages red again and one has a backward 'time warp' of some ten years or more. The engines are Compound 4-4-0 No.41088 and 'Jubilee' 4-6-0 No.45662 Kempenfelt.

The train itself is not recorded but is thought likely to have been a through service from Bristol and the West of England to the West Riding.

21

Treacy did not take locomotive portraits quite as often as moving trains, but when he did, they were rarely stereotyped since he almost always tried to inject pictorial quality into the pure record. Typical is this view of humble Class 2P 4-4-0 No.M671 at Chester, just after Nationalisation. The engine is plain black and is only on a routine stopping train, but in his view, it takes on quite a noble aspect. The 'M' prefix, just visible on the cabside, was part of a short-lived early BR renumbering scheme and only lasted for a few months.

This early BR view dates from 1949 and shows 'Royal Scot' 4-6-0 No.46163 Civil Service Rifleman departing through Hampstead Road bridge on the 'down' fast line out of Euston. This engine was one of only 28 'Scots' to remain unrebuilt at the close of the LMS period and, livery apart, this sort of scene was re-enacted at this spot daily for more than ten years, very little changing save for livery. The carriages are mostly now in BR red and cream and the engine is in experimental BR livery, lined black with LNWR style lining. The engine is based at Bushbury and the train is likely to be a Birmingham and Wolverhampton express.

The exit from Chester where it threads the city walls en route to Holyhead had some parallels with that from Liverpool Lime Street, so it is not to be wondered that Treacy explored its pictorial potential. The main view, taken in 1948, shows rebuilt 'Royal Scot' No.46127 Old Contemptibles in experimental LNWR style livery leaving with the 'down' 'Irish Mail'. The reader may well feel he has seen this picture somewhere before, but the smaller view shows the one which is usually published, taken a few weeks or months later when the same engine was more grimy. It had then also acquired its proper BR pattern front numberplate not to mention a new position on the cabside for its power classification marking! One does rather wonder how much it cost to make all these piffling changes which Treacy recorded so well.

On a general point, maybe due to the fairly small size photographic reproductions in those days, Treacy seems to have been quite fond of cropping his pictures tight to the engine but for my money, the wider view is preferable, largely because the whole scene is present, thus giving a better sense of scale between the train and its setting. It is, of course, a very subjective business; here, readers can judge for themselves.

This first general look at the subject is concluded by a powerful and typically Treacy impression of main line steam in action on the northern hills in the high summer of 1948. The LMS had given way to the new order but Stanier's 'Duchesses' were just getting back to their peak. This is de-streamlined No.46247 City of Liverpool on the 'up' 'Mid-Day Scot' towards Shap. The engine is still in LMS colours, as is more than half the train, itself composed of vehicles from all three LMS design periods.

24

Chapter 2

The LMS Environment

In the early days of railway photography, it was customary to fill the viewfinder of the camera with the main subject of the picture, be it locomotive, train or whatever. Treacy was different. While he may not have been the first to incorporate something of the environment in which the subject matter was based, he was one of the pioneers and almost certainly the finest exponent of the deliberately taken view in which the setting as well as the 'mobile hardware' played a vital part. During his LMS period, he was, if not alone, very much the leader of what, in retrospect, can be seen to have been a new 'school' of thought. Prior to Treacy, the environmental aspect of a picture was either absent or, if present at all, more often than not an accidental by-product. Treacy regularly made it the central feature.

It was this aspect of his photography which first attracted me so I make no apology, as a professional geographer, for starting in this area. Railways are, first and foremost, economic arteries of communication and their physical relationship to the many regions through which they pass is not haphazard. In all cases, the landscape, be it urban or rural, was there first and the railway had to be tailored to suit. In the case of heavily built over areas, such as our major towns and cities, the railway often had to be squeezed in, fighting for space amongst many other aspects of human endeavour. Out in the open country, the nature of the physical landscape itself (hills, valleys etc) was probably the overriding factor while in other areas it may have been a subtle mix of both constraints. Eric Treacy seemed instinctively to understand this fact, although he never formalised it in the form of an academic analysis. No matter, the end product was there for all to see in his pictures. He even adopted what, in contemporary context must have seemed an outrageous practice of actually taking railway pictures without trains!

But the railway environment is not just the landscape and setting; it is also the more immediate surroundings of the system itself. Treacy recognised this too. From conversations with him it became clear to me that while he never worried himself about the precise minutiae and probably would not have known the difference between a Midland or an LNWR water column (!), he was acutely aware of the contribution which such things could make to the total scene. Freed from the dedicated enthusiast's obsession with pedantic detail, he let his artistic 'eye' dominate and thus opened up refreshing new ways of looking at things. Who, for example, in pre-Treacy days, could have dreamed of the artistic possibilities of the gloomy and smoke-ridden cuttings and tunnels between Liverpool Lime Street and Edge Hill? Treacy did just this, so much so in this particular case that I have elected to

This undated view of a northbound freight train traversing the Lune Gorge in pre-M6 days is characteristic of Treacy's landscape approach. It could have been taken at any time between the 1930s and the 1950s; the Stanier Class 5 and its train were 'ever presents' during that period. However, its main function seems to be to show the utter insignificance of the old LNWR main line when set against the backdrop of this huge landscape. The pictorial composition is superb with the focal point (the white smoke) sitting not dead centre but more or less on the intersection of thirds – the strongest point in the view. From here, the eye is led left to right into the picture and then, by virtue of the darker shadows in the railway cutting and on the horizon (right hand edges), one's attention is moved onto the barren fell side and the sky. The bank of trees and the hillside valley (lower and upper left edges) then prevent the eye leaving the picture, thus completing the full circle. It is simple but satisfying and really conveys the sense of 'place' – a characteristic Treacy attribute which, one feels, did not happen by accident.

The former Lancashire & Yorkshire main line between the red and white rose counties rarely strayed far from the concentration of urban development and Treacy homed in on Sowerby Bridge at an early stage during his West Riding ministry. He often favoured an elevated viewpoint and this picture, taken looking eastward in early BR days, is typical. In just one view, he has managed to encapsulate the complexities of the railway scene with more than a hint of the difficult physical terrain and urban complexity which the LYR had to encounter. Whether consciously or not, he even chose to wait until the train was headed by an ex-LYR 2-4-2T locomotive, the carriages themselves being of LMS design.

(Opposite) The industrial landscapes of both Lancashire and the old West Riding of Yorkshire, particularly the latter, were characterised by a distinctive mix of close packed urban development in the valleys and wide open hillsides separating these zones. The LMS Railway, in the shape of its various pre-1923 constituents, was well and truly represented in this industrial scene. This evocative view of the Yorkshire end of Standedge Tunnel on the former LNWR main line between Huddersfield and Manchester shows it to perfection right at the point where urban concentration has given way to a rather more rural environment. The eye wanders happily about the picture noting the contrast between the substantial 19th century railway engineering, the earlier and less flamboyant style of the Huddersfield Narrow Canal and, in the distance, the dry stone walls and weavers' cottages of an earlier age. It is truly the essence of the northern railway environment and yet it is also a real picture in the absolute sense. One almost feels that the presence of a moving train would distract from one's appreciation of the scene. Yet note how cleverly Treacy has injected just a modicum of human activity into his composition by means of the diesel shunter and its crew in the lower right foreground. The picture is not dated but the LMS did have diesel shunters and the bullhead track denotes an early date.

devote a whole section to this one particular area, which is why it does not feature in this chapter.

It is a moot point whether Treacy's environmental pictures are better or worse for having trains intrude – it all depends on one's particular point of view I suppose – but what can be said is that at their best they prompted many later photographers to emulate his example. I have spoken with many of them and they all speak with one voice as to his inspirational qualities. But it was, in fact, the LMS Railway which became the first focus of his attention in this respect and in this sense it set the pattern for most which followed. In this selection I have, therefore, tried to show something of the way in which Eric Treacy first set about the task.

29

These pictures represent the first example of many in this survey which illustrate how Treacy captured the changing LMS scene without perhaps realising it. They were both taken at Sowerby Bridge, from much the same position as the previous view but this time looking West. At first glance they seem almost identical, but they repay careful study. The upper view shows a very early BR scene of pure LMS character, save for the train livery. The engine is a Stanier Class 5XP Jubilee, No.45717 Dauntless and the carriages are all to LMS design. The second view is later and does not really qualify as pure LMS. True, the former War Department 2-8-0s, represented by the train engine in the foreground, were designed by an LMS man – as, indeed, was the Ivatt 2-6-0 on the passenger train in the platform – but note that the delapidated LMS station and platform canopies of the first view have been replaced, as have the foreground telephone wires and poles. Even the factory door (lower right corner) has changed.

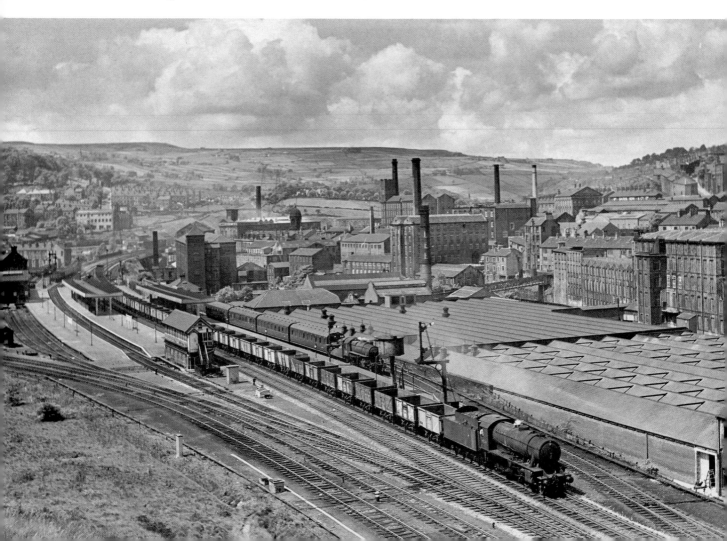

The North Wales main line of the former LNWR was not the most visited of Treacy's LMS locations but he did give it his favour from time to time. In this view of Conway Castle we see the pure landscape photographer at work. There is nothing particularly remarkable about it save that he did not bother to wait until a train was passing. The juxtaposition of Edwardian castle and the sympathetically designed Robert Stephenson tubular bridge seems to have been sufficient inspiration for this crisp view.

From time to time Treacy seemed almost to subdue his pictorial approach in favour of a more clinical recording of the scene. This view at the former LNWR Llandudno Junction is characteristic. At first glance it seems less than riveting but his placement of the various static features still shows a sense of artistry – one cannot seriously believe that the dominance of the water column on the right was accidental. However, thirty or forty years later, one is also conscious of the long gone bullhead track with its LNWR chairs, the lovely little LNWR gantry with its semaphore shunting signals and the detail of the point rodding and signal wires in the right foreground. 'En passant', Treacy also managed to capture the essential difference between the platform mounted and more conventional LNWR water columns. One can be fairly sure that he did not intend this, but how fortunate that he was there!

31

Robert Stephenson's Britannia tubular bridge, which carried the LMS (ex-LNWR) Holyhead main line across the Menai Straits, is justly famous and has been much recorded by railway photographers – mostly from the trackside with a train emerging from the tubes themselves. Treacy was not, as far as is known, tempted to follow this hackneyed approach. Instead, his only known picture of this structure was very much a tribute to its essential engineering quality. Given the traumatic fire disaster of 1970 and the subsequent rebuilding of the structure as a combined rail/road bridge a few years later, this (undated) picture now takes on the role of a valuable historical record of a unique Victorian achievement.

One of the joys of sitting by the lineside, waiting for a train to come along, is well captured here by a fine record shot of Dillicar troughs on the Lancaster and Carlisle main line of the LMS (ex-LNWR). One can almost sense that the photographer, striving for something to occupy the time, has decided that the combination of this unique feature of railway operation, plus the undoubted grandeur of the scenery, is well worth a bit of effort. The picture cannot be dated but the flat bottomed rail infers early BR. The LMS equivalent would have been little different.

Shap Bank was a favourite Treacy location but it is less well known that he also recorded the hill in train-less mode. This is a catch point on the northbound ascent, complete with LNWR notice board and only revealed as early BR by virtue of the flat bottomed track on the down road.

Scout Green Box – a famous marker point on Shap Bank – was a fine place to watch trains and Treacy spent much time there. This simple view, devoid of much detail, save for the railway itself and the wild surrounding landscape, says everything that needs to be said about this famous interactive location between man's endeavour and the natural environment. It changed little over the years until the motorway and electric railway era – this view dates from the early 1950s.

(Opposite, above) The old Glasgow & South Western route of the LMS between Carlisle and Scotland's largest city was not particularly renowned as Treacy territory until BR days, but he did eventually get there and this lovely peaceful view of the celebrated Ballochmyle Viaduct can hardly have changed for decades. The picture is undated but it matters not in context. Treacy's unerring sense of pictorialism has managed to capture, to perfection, the subtle harmony between the man made and the natural scene. Neither would be very inspiring without the other, but the blend of the two enhances both. It is beside the point to mention that when built, this lovely arch was the largest man made masonry structure of its kind anywhere in the world. One senses that Treacy just knew . . .

Beattock Bank, between Carlisle and Glasgow on the old Caledonian line of the LMS, was a very difficult place to record with the camera – and still is for that matter. The main problem is its geographical alignment in relation to the direction of the sun and the disposition of the hill masses. Nothing daunted, Treacy tackled the problem, for it was a truly inspiring place in which to witness man against the elements. The records do not tell us when he first went there but his achievements in later BR days were formidable. This view shows an early BR scene, almost certainly unchanged from the LMS era, wherein a Caledonian 0-6-0 goods engine gets to grips with the north-bound ascent. Paradoxically, with the benefit of some forty years of hindsight, almost the most interesting feature is the nature of the A74 main road in the foreground, nearly devoid of traffic and certainly not the dual carriageway death trap of the 1980s. Maybe we went wrong somewhere, but Treacy recorded the event for posterity!

(Opposite, below) In the fullness of time, Eric Treacy finally found himself at that LMS (ex-Highland Railway) outpost, the Kyle of Lochalsh. We do not know exactly when, but it was certainly post-Nationalisation. Fortunately, the erstwhile LMS scene had hardly changed and Treacy still felt disposed to record the total environment as well as the trains. In this view he concentrated on the familiar sight of a MacBrayne ship Loch Seaforth at the quayside which, together with the distant hills of the Ise of Skye and the railway sidings in the foreground, encapsulated the scene – one can almost smell the fish in those boxes in the right foreground!

I first met Eric Treacy at the personal level in context of my researches into the Settle and Carlisle main line of the LMS (ex-Midland Railway). It subsequently transpired that he considered this particular bit of railway to be his favourite line and therein began our friendship. I do not therefore propose to apologise for concluding this section of the book by a rather more detailed look at the way in which he saw his quite unique example of the LMS scene. It truly encapsulates the whole of his approach and we start, in a modest way, by looking at a typical record shot of Settle station. Apart from the incursion of a few bits of BR flat-bottomed track and some LMS/BR upper quadrant signals, this is pure Midland Railway, water tower, architecture and all.

(Opposite) This is a case where the train helps! The view is in Ribblesdale, just above Horton, where the Settle and Carlisle line traverses the wide open spaces prior to its real encounter with the high hills. Pen-y-Ghent is the mountain in the background and the train, a northbound freight headed by a Class 4 0-6-0, is just about the only man-made feature in this wild and barren landscape.

The Ribble gorge at Sherriff Brow. There is no train in sight and nothing is particularly remarkable save for the sheer crispness of the image and the pleasant composition of the whole picture. One does, however, suspect that the overhanging foreground branches and the platelayer and his dog were not entirely accidental!

(Opposite) Everyone has heard of Ribblehead Viaduct, but before Treacy, there were few who would have dared take this sort of picture in the context of railways. Heaven knows when it was taken or what the engine was – but does it really matter? The essential ingredient of this picture is the sheer vastness of the environment and the audacity of those men of the Midland Railway who tackled it head on so as to get their line of railway through. Only Treacy would, at the time, have had the nerve to take his camera so far back from the railway as to get the local road and stream prominent in the foreground, thus relegating the railway almost to second place . . . but it surely works.

This rather more conventional view shows a tumble engineer's train, composed of an ex-LNWR carriage, a handful of LMS wagons and ex-MR Class 4F 0-6-0 No. 3922 en route between Ribblehead Viaduct and Blea Moor Tunnel. The summit of Pen-y-Ghent figures on the left, the flanks of Ingleborough are seen on the right and more than half the picture features a quite magnificent sky scene. Was Treacy lucky or did he wait – who knows? All one can say is that the essence of 'railway' is caught in views such as this.

This is yet another example of Treacy's 'trainless' approach. He did in fact capture much the same view with a freight train in the picture but somehow, this study of the northbound approach to Blea Moor Tunnel with nothing save the railway itself together with the minuscule figures of the platelayers representing the human element, seems to capture the essence of the Settle – Carlisle as well as any picture of a steam train.

(Overleaf) This majestic view of Ribblehead shows Treacy's railway landscape approach at its magnificent best and simply had to be included for although taken in the mid-1950s, it is a truly timeless scene. The composition itself is well-nigh perfect with the train, viaduct, signal and the distant mass of Pen-y-Ghent all forming a powerful visual group at the strong position in the picture. There is no way it can have been taken by accident – but goodness only knows how many times Treacy may have gone back to get the right

combination of light and sky in conjunction with the train in the right position.

It was not until late in the preparation of the book that I realised that this was a BR train not an LMS one, made up of a mixture of LMS and BR stock. The all-red carriage colours had fooled me. However, it is the one exception I have allowed myself in terms of 'hardware'; for the record, the 'down' 'Waverley' (BR descendant of the LMS 'Thames-Forth Express'), double headed by Class 5 and 'Jubilee' 4-6-0s, probably c1957/8.

39

Dent (ex-MR) was the highest LMS station in England and Eric Treacy well and truly fell under its spell. It was, in truth, a somewhat crazy place to put a station and its remoteness is well captured here. Yet again the precise dates are unknown but the scene is pure LMS. Indeed, but for the Horwich 2-6-0 No. 42774 on the southbound freight in one of the views, the pictures are almost timeless. As always, Treacy's sense of pictorial composition is superb. Note how in one case the locomotive itself occupies the strong position at the intersection of thirds, while on the passive view, the grouping of station building, platelayer's shelter and signal box fulfil the same role. This was surely no accident. Others have copied it since but none have done it better.

This road between Garsdale and Ais Gill has become familiar to a whole generation of railway enthusiasts in the 1980s as they join in the mad and crazy scramble to get a better view of steam excursions on the Settle and Carlisle, but how many have stopped for a moment to consider the wild yet placid beauty of the total scene? Very few I imagine; but Treacy did and this c1950 view is one of his very best efforts. Yet again, no train intrudes but one senses that this was no sudden impulse picture either. The position of the car, the grouping of the tree clusters to left and right centre and the way in which the road itself leads one gently into the scene all betoken the master craftsman. Wild Boar Fell in the background gives the all-essential 'stop' to the scene and even the small human figure on the road is placed to perfection – was it perhaps Mrs Treacy? Whatever the true story, the end product is a superb evocation of a railway in its natural setting and one could not ask for more.

43

Although he went there before the war, Treacy seems not to have discovered the full potential of Euston Station and its approaches until just about the time of Nationalisation. He usually went for departures rather than arrivals – presumably because the engines were likely to be working harder – and found a nice little spot just to the north of the Hampstead Road bridge and kept going back there. This view, taken in the summer of 1948, shows rebuilt 'Royal Scot' 4-6-0 No.46122 Royal Ulster Rifleman, departing with an unidentified express. The 9A (Longsight) shed code suggests a homeward bound Manchester train. The only carriage visible is still wearing LMS colours as is the locomotive (a plain unlined black – no doubt its original utility livery, received when rebuilt in 1945), but the BR number has appeared on smokebox and cabside.

Chapter 3

Some Favourite Locations

It seems a logical follow-on after noting Eric Treacy's view of the LMS environment to consider some of his favourite locations on that system. In all honesty, there were not too many of them and it is somewhat conjectural at this range in time whether they were chosen through force of circumstances or for more subtle reasons. During the LMS period proper – and for a few years afterwards – he seems to have been content with a handful of locations in the north together with the odd foray, presumably for ecclesiastical reasons, to London. There is a yawning gap between London and Lancashire which Treacy never really explored until later days – and even then not very much. This of course, excluded much of the LMS heartland but at the same time, there was just enough variety of location to enable him to capture the essence of the railway in most of its moods.

Given that generalisations are always a bit dangerous, it seems probable that Treacy had two specific preferred types of place – wild open country or right in the thick of the urban scene. Nearly all his best work seems to fall into one of these two classifications. Of them, the Settle and Carlisle was probably the single most favoured open air venue and, without doubt, the exit from Liverpool was his most visited urban location. The former has already been examined and the latter is the subject of its own special study in Chapter 6, so this selection concentrates on some of the other places.

As always, Treacy regularly revisited his favourite places. One cannot be sure whether this was because he had a persistent vision of the definitive view at that location or whether it was a consequence of having relatively little time to spare. After all, if one has only an hour or two it makes abundant sense to go back to a place whose photographic potential is known. Whatever the precise reasons, the record of change made the end product worthwhile.

This section of the book is predominantly about locations, but it would be wrong to stop there, for Treacy's pictures rarely covered but one aspect of the scene. Some indeed were pure records of places but many other views, while characteristic of the locations he chose, were much more besides, giving much valuable supplementary information about the railway itself. In the captions, therefore, I have chosen also to mention some of the other interesting points which the pictures reveal, hopefully establishing by so-doing, a few of the themes which later chapters will expand.

(Opposite) In this second 1948 study, Crewe based de-streamlined 'Coronation' Class 4-6-2 No.46236 City of Bradford, gets under way with a real mixed bag of assets! The first four coaches of the train, all in LMS colours are, respectively: Stanier c1940 rebuild of a pre-1930 brake composite, 'all steel' LMS 1920s style open third, fully wood panelled LMS 1920s style open third and an ex-LNWR corridor composite. The engine itself, which was, incidentally, the only LMS 4-6-2 chosen for the 1948 BR locomotive exchanges, is in the fully lined 1946 LMS black express passenger livery wearing full BR insignia in LMS style (including the front numberplate). The LNWR shunting signals, also prominent in the previous view – did not last much longer and Treacy has subtly moved a little further away from the bridge to get more of the environment in shot, even managing to capture a London Transport trolley bus on the bridge itself.

45

Most of Treacy's pre-war work at the London end of the LMS seems to have been confined to the Kilburn High Road area. This c1937 shot is 'Princess' Class 4-6-2 No.6210 Lady Patricia, *with the north-bound 'Mid-Day Scot' express. The second vehicle is a twelve wheel Stanier diner and the third a pre-Stanier 1928 vintage semi-open first.*

This second view of another 'Princess' at Kilburn High Road, now No.6203 Princess Margaret Rose probably shows the same train as the previous view but a few months, or maybe a year or so later. The leading carriage is still a Stanier brake third but is of slightly later vintage with deeper height upper window ventilators. The positions of the twelve wheel diner and semi-open first have been transposed and the latter is now one of the 1930 low waisted variants.

By 1950, the new BR liveries were well to the fore but the basic 'hardware' operating out of Euston had not changed too much. This is well shown in this fine action shot of Princess Margaret Rose again, now No.46203 and seen climbing Camden Bank with 13 or 14 bogies in tow. Most carriages are of Stanier style but the second is a wooden bodied composite of pre-1930 vintage while the third one is, for some reason, of GWR origin, maybe even still in chocolate and cream. There appears to be only one vehicle retaining LMS livery but the locomotive is still in LMS condition – ie with domeless boiler. The engine is none too clean but may well have been BR blue.

Treacy loved the pre-war streamliners and he certainly chased the blue and silver 'Coronation Scot' trains to good effect. This view, however, is not, quite what it seems. It is, of course, one of many taken at Kilburn in 1937-8 and shows No.6221 Queen Elizabeth *with an express undoubtedly bound for Glasgow. The W97 reporting number is, however, that of the Saturday 'Mid-Day Scot' which, on that day only, consisted of the blue and silver 'Coronation Scot' set augmented by general service stock. My guess is that Treacy may have been in London for some weekend ecclesiastical affair and took time out on Saturday afternoon for a few hours!*

(Opposite) Preston was one of Treacy's earliest locations and he regularly returned. He also met with very good fortune in his 'camera spotting' during his limited time there. This mid-1948 view of a southbound express hauled by de-streamlined 4-6-2 No.46227 Duchess of Devonshire, *shows one of only four ex-streamliners to wear the short lived experimental dark blue BR livery with LNWR type lining. Not only that, but he has caught another typically LMS mixed bag of carriages, all still in company livery. The second and fifth vehicles are ex-LNWR, the fourth and sixth are pre-1933 LMS standards and the bulk of the rest are of Stanier pattern.*

North now to Preston at the point where the West Coast main line diverged from the Blackpool route (right). Although the train, headed by 'Princess' 4-6-2 No.6211 Queen Maud, *is photographed at quite a steep angle, such is the clarity of Treacy's photography that we can clearly see that it is, once again, our old friend the 'Mid-Day Scot' last seen at Kilburn with brake third, twelve wheel diner and semi-open first leading. This time the brake third is the later type but the semi-open is of the earlier pattern. Astonishingly, Treacy recorded all three formation variations within a twelve-month. The fact that in all three cases it was also 'Princess' hauled suggests that the period was 1937-8 before the streamlined 'Coronation' class had been multiplied beyond the first five examples. A few years later, this sort of job would often be performed by the newer 4-6-2s.*

Treacy first discovered the Lake District in the 1930s. This evocative view at Penrith in high summer c1937, is typical of many he took which, quite unconsciously, recorded many now-vanished aspects of the railway scene. On the left, Fowler 2-6-4T No.2393 sets off with a local train for Keswick, having undoubtedly made its connection with the simultaneously departing southbound express, probably from Aberdeen and Perth, headed by Crewe based 'Royal Scot' No.6164 The Artists Rifleman. *On the right, an unidentified Class 4F 0-6-0 bearing stopping train headlamp waits with a train whose leading carriage is one of the high seating capacity Stanier open third class brakes. The*

smokebox reporting number suggests some form of special excursion and the use of a 4F on passenger duty serves as a reminder that these so-called freight engines were often called upon for passenger work at busy times.

The main train too is interesting. It has a container wagon behind the tender and at each end of the carriage section, which contains the usual mixture of 'ancient and modern' stock, is a full brake, the leading example being of ex-LYR origin. Note, however, the milk tank in second position, in this case a road trailer mounted on a six-wheel flat wagon. We shall meet it again, or something like it, more than once in ensuing pages.

(Opposite, above) Another more than normally interesting picture at this favourite Treacy location of Penrith shows LMS standard Class 4P Compound 4-4-0 No.1101, based at Newton Heath, Manchester, setting off for its home base c1937 with a light five-coach express whose formation is distinctly peculiar. The first three vehicles are Stanier corridors but to no known standard make-up for a short set viz: brake composite (brake end inwards), third, brake third. Bringing up the rear however are a non-corridor ex-LYR brake third and what looks like a turn of century ex-LNWR arc roof corridor third. Add to this the raft of cattle wagons plus ex-LNWR water column on the right and the string of sheeted down open goods wagons in the left distance and one has a perfect evocation of the LMS of the later 1930s. The train engine itself is one of the rather rarer examples fitted with an exhaust steam injector and still carries the pre-1936 livery with black shaded gold insignia and small(ish) numbers on the cabside.

Another LMS standard Compound, this time right hand drive No.1068 of Leeds (Holbeck), leaves Carlisle after the war with a train bound for the Settle and Carlisle line. This picture has been published before mainly to show the old Carlisle Citadel station roof. However, when compared with the previous view at Penrith it also reveals other aspects of ten years of change within but one locomotive class. The engine, of course, is now filthy unlined black but it also has a replacement Stanier chimney (quite common), a 1936 pattern front numberplate (less usual), no coal rails on the tender (not much coal either for a trip to Leeds over that particular route!) and no exhaust steam injector.

Carlisle station in 1948/9. The scene is pure LMS but the new BR livery abounds, the most interesting aspect of it being the experimental use of LNWR lining which was applied to several Holbeck based Class 5XP 4-6-0s including No.45569 Tasmania. Some were apple green, which looked ghastly, but this example was probably a black one in the style later used by BR for its mixed traffic engines. Needless to say, Treacy was there!

Treacy reckoned the rebuilt 'Royal Scots' to be amongst his favourite engines and he certainly captured most of them on film over a period of some twenty or more years. He took many splendid studies of them leaving Carlisle, bound for former Glasgow & South Western territory with trains from the old Midland route. This is one of his best, Leeds based No.6117 Welsh Guardsman en route for Glasgow in 1947, immaculately finished in the full 1946 LMS express livery – a very smart turnout indeed when clean and one which suited the engines very well, especially in pre-smoke deflector days. The train is the 'Thames-Clyde Express' – see also Chapter 5.

'Treacy's LMS' hardly extended into Scotland during Company days, but he began to explore its potential so soon after Nationalisation as to be able to record many pure 'LMS' scenes, some of which it would be a pity to exclude from this selection. This 1948 view of Beattock Bank shows that he started in his usual way by first having a go at the environment. This is a typical loose-coupled LMS freight composed largely of wooden bodied open wagons, headed by an unidentified Class 5 4-6-0 in early BR colours and banked, probably, by an ex-Caledonian Railway 0-4-4T.

This classic shot of a northbound express on Beattock Bank cannot be dated with precision but is unlikely to have been much later than 1950 – the year when the Polmadie shed code became 66A – for apart from this and the train livery, everything is pure LMS. Change it all to crimson lake and the time could easily have been fifteen years earlier. It is, of course, Princess Margaret Rose again, still with LMS domeless boiler and in charge of an almost obscenely tidy set of Stanier carriages.

These two c1950/51 views at Princes Street Station, the former Caledonian Railway terminus in Edinburgh now, alas, gone for ever, show a very common Treacy technique, that of recording a sequence of activity. In the first picture, ex-CR Pickersgill 4-4-0 No.54503 awaits departure with what at first sight seems like a humdrum non-corridor local train; but it carries express headlamps and it takes the second view of its actual departure to reveal that much of the train consists of modern Stanier gangwayed stock. The train was probably bound for Larbert or Carstairs and the leading pair of carriages, both third class, may well have been strengtheners – a common enough LMS practice. The pictures show much other period detail, for example, LMS upper quadrant signal arms on ex-CR posts, contemporary bullhead trackwork and the early BR painting style used on locomotives, main line and suburban stock. For carriage enthusiasts, we even have the number of one of them, non-corridor third class No.SC11143M, one of a hundred built at Wolverton in 1928 and still very much in original state.

54

These somewhat similar thematic pictures to the previous pair, show that other long vanished LMS terminus in Scotland – former Glasgow & South Western, St Enoch Station with its noble arched roof. They should perhaps, have been omitted from this survey as they date from the late 1950s (note the post-1956 BR tender emblem), but they have been included because almost everything, station and train, is still purely LMS; even the notice boards carry LMS lettering along their tops, albeit now painted out. The train itself is of a very common GSW area pattern in LMS times – a set of non-corridor LMS standard carriages hauled by a standard Class 2P 4-4-0 No.40579 based at Ardrossan to where the train was probably going. Note the continued use of the LMS Scottish style semaphore route indicator on the front lamp iron, a practice dating from Caledonian times. This sort of scene could have been witnessed here for nigh on thirty years for the engine was built in 1928 and the carriages are all of pre-Stanier vintage, the leading one being a steel panelled example from c1931-2, the others being some four or five years older.

Along with the line from Lime Street to Wavertree, the northbound ascent of Shap Bank was probably Treacy's most cele-brated single location. This is one of his all-time classics and I don't much care how many times it has been seen before, it will surely stand repetition. In fact, it has not been published for a generation – blue and silver streamlined 4-6-2 No.6222 Queen Mary *on the 'down' 'Coronation Scot' in 1937.*

(Opposite, above) This everyday scene of a northbound freight being banked up Shap could be witnessed dozens of times every 24 hours until the later 1960s – but Treacy has invested it with real pictorial quality. Fowler 2-6-4T No.2396 actually pushes the eye into the picture as well as the train up the hill! For the record, he also captured one of the few engines of this class to be repainted in 1936/7 with the short-lived sans-serif LMS pattern insignia.

(Opposite, below) Ten or more years later, Treacy was still tackling Shap with the same vigour as its engines! This is an early BR view of the 10.05 Euston-Perth train behind 'Jubilee' Class 5XP 4-6-0 No.45578 United Provinces, then based at Carlisle. The train, in a mixture of LMS and BR colours, is an uncharacteristically tidy formation of Stanier stock save for the leading carriage, a c1928 period open third and probably an added 'strengthener'.

The southbound ascent of Shap was less famous than the 1:75 northbound hill but probably more onerous since it was longer and one often had a 'cold' engine from Carlisle. Most of Treacy's pictures on this demanding bit of line date from later BR days but he was there from time to time before the war as this c1937 view of 'Royal Scot' 4-6-0 No.6104 Scottish Borderer at Thrimby reveals. In this case, a Glasgow (Polmadie) engine is working through to England, still with its Caledonian Railway pattern of route indicator in position over the centre lamp-iron.

Leeds City was one of the locations which Treacy covered comprehensively, particularly in the five or six years after his arrival in the West Riding. This is a c1950 view, still pure LMS save for the new liveries. The train is a Scottish bound departure from the old Midland part of the station behind Carlisle based Class 5XP 4-6-0 No.45716 Swiftsure. Amongst the many details of this typical 'railway' scene may be noted the LMS signal arms on ex-MR posts, the considerable degree of track complexity (mostly in bullhead rail) and the great number of carriages and vans of all descriptions occupying the platforms.

Even when Treacy was going for a pure picture, he often managed to record much history, often of a very transient nature. This is one such, a 1948 northbound departure from Leeds for Carlisle. It was taken a few hundred yards further out than the previous view, at the point where the Midland route turns right for Holbeck and the Aire Valley. The train engine is one of Holbeck's stalwart 'Jubilees', No.45565 Victoria, *seen in the short-lived BR experimental apple green livery with LNWR style lining – not the happiest choice of colour schemes. However, it is beautifully 'framed' by three sets of original MR signals, not to mention the old MR signal box.*

After the West Coast Main Line (including its Lancashire offshoots) and the Midland route north of Leeds, Treacy's most visited main line location was probably the Chester and Holyhead line. Yet again he often managed to explore it during the interesting transition period from LMS to BR. This first view, taken at Chester late in 1947, shows newly rebuilt 'Royal Scot' No.6115 Scots Guardsman, *the only LMS rebuild to be given smoke deflectors, leaving with a parcels train. He also took a more formal picture of the engine at this time, included in the next chapter, but the interest here is more purely railway. Note that four of the first five vehicles are either for horses or prize cattle, a traffic no longer carried by rail. LNWR signals and signal box are prominent and the lack of depot allocation plate on the engine smokebox, together with its almost ex-shops finish, suggests it was on some form of 'running in' duty.*

In this 1949 view, a Llandudno based Compound 4-4-0, so filthy as to defy identification, leaves Chester with the 4.28pm Crewe to Bangor train below another fine array of ex-LNWR signals. The train formation is, once more, rather interesting. The leading carriage is an LMS fully panelled brake composite of the 1920s, followed by two quite modern GWR third class carriages which still seem to be chocolate and cream, while the last identifiable vehicles are two more 1920s LMS types, a corridor composite and, probably, an open third.

Contrary to popular belief, the LMS did not always use tank engines for shunting duties. Often, anything in steam was considered appropriate and here at Bangor, c1950, former Lancashire & Yorkshire 0-6-0 No.52119 demonstrates that old habits died hard after Nationalisation. It was based at Bangor, presumably for local freight duties in the district, but in this view it appears to be positioning a set of carriages, including dining cars. The dining formation itself is the very typical LMS pairing of twelve wheel kitchen/first class plus eight wheel open third.

This chapter has given many examples of the way in which Treacy recorded the changeover from LMS to BR and this concluding example continues in this vein. It is a 1948 shot of the 'up' 'Irish Mail' leaving Holyhead behind rebuilt 'Royal Scot' No.46166 London Rifle Brigade. Only the new number betrays that this is not a pure LMS picture for the engine is in 1946 company livery and all carriages are in LMS colours. One feels that perhaps inevitably, Treacy has also managed, without really trying, to record more than just a nice picture. The leading full brake is a type much associated with this working, but the photographer was there when it was one of the interesting and none too common post-war rebuilds of pre-war passenger carrying coaches. Even the leading brake first is unusual, one of the small batch of experimental 'all steel' coaches built in 1931!

This view of No.6143 Mail, is almo[st]
certainly one of Treacy's earliest ev[er]
railway photographs and cannot be la[ter]
than 1934, the year in which the engine w[as]
re-named The South Staffordshire Re[gi]-
ment. It may even be earlier, for at th[at]
time the engines were in process of receivi[ng]
smoke deflector shields and the date [at]
which No.6143 received them is not know[n].
The lack of depot shedplate on t[he]
smokebox does however, support a c19[34]
date, just prior to the renumbering of LM[S]
motive power depots to the familiar 'distr[ict]
number plus suffix letter' arrangement.

The commonist mid-1930s form of t[he]
'Scots' was with angle-topped smoke d[e-]
flectors, Fowler tenders (now with co[al]
rails) and red LMS livery with g[old]
insignia, shaded black in the post-19[33]
style. These features are all shown on t[he]
view of No.6156 The South Wa[les]
Borderer climbing Shap unassisted with [a]
13 coach train, yet also blowing off stea[m]
at the same time. The leading full brake [is]
of LNWR origin and there is anoth[er]
ex-LNWR carriage fifth from the rear b[ut]
surprisingly for this early date (1935[?])
most of the train is new Stanier stock.

Chapter 4

The Changing Face of LMS Express Steam

There can be no real doubt that Treacy was a 'main line' sort of person and a large proportion of his output was addressed to the business of capturing the main line steam train in all its moods. He took thousands of pictures of trains on the move and amongst them, express passenger workings probably took pride of place. In consequence, his pictures give an unparalleled record of change in this specific area. The next chapter concentrates on the trains themselves but in this selection, the emphasis is upon the locomotive.

Treacy liked big express engines and, as far as can be judged, the newer they were the better. Not for him the pursuit of superannuated relics of the pre-group era, that was left to others. He went for the mainstream stuff and at this range in time it is interesting to speculate why. I have the feeling that it was not through any distaste for the products of a past era but was more bound up with the work which the various classes were likely to be found performing during his time, for his own writings reveal that he was striving to capture the steam engine working hard. In the very nature of things the most onerous duties would be given to the newest and most powerful machines so the concentration on the latest types is not too surprising. In a different age he would probably have been chasing Georges and Claughtons on the West Coast Main Line, recording the exploits of Midland compounds over the Long Drag or following the activities of Caledonian 4-4-0s in Scotland. As it was, his camera, during LMS days, found itself mostly pointing at the latest products of the Company and it is with these that this chapter is concerned.

Now it is tolerably certain that Eric Treacy was not deliberately trying to make a definitive historical record but, in the event, that is one of the things he actually achieved as far as the LMS standard express classes were concerned. Simply by concentrating on this one area of activity, he managed, purely by chance, to capture just about every significant change which took place. What makes it more interesting is the fact that there is a lack of self-conscious 'poseness' about his record. He was always seeking for a 'picture' and even when he chose to forsake the train and concentrate purely on the locomotive, his sense of pictorialism rarely let him down.

This selection concentrates on but three groups of engines, the 'Royal Scots' (the first purely LMS designed express type), the two varieties of Stanier 4-6-2s and the so-called '5XP' 4-6-0 classes. Some of the pictures are semi-formal locomotive portraits but many more show them at work. In this latter case I have chosen train pictures where, in my judgement, the engine interest outweighs the other aspects in the picture. However, Treacy's

pictures were often so full of other peripheral 'goodies' that in many cases it would be impossible and, indeed, undesirable not to mention them. This is always a difficulty when trying to categorise a Treacy photograph. Thus, although this selection is a quite genuine survey of the changing express locomotive scene, it also contains more than a little of the ancillary detail which his pictures so often reveal.

Treacy, of course, went on recording LMS steam for another decade or more after the BR influence began to make itself very obvious and one could equally well find as many or more of his pictures which cover their last fifteen years, but this group of views keeps pretty strictly to the 1934-50 parameters, with but a few obvious and necessary exceptions – and there is not a single domed boiler 'Lizzie' in sight! For ease of understanding, the pictures are arranged by classes and, within each class, are grouped chronologically.

As years passed, the limited coal capacity of the Fowler tenders caused them to be exchanged with new Stanier 4,000 gallon 9 ton tenders actually built for use with 'Jubilee' Class 5XP 4-6-0s. No.6119 Lancashire Fusilier is seen thus in this attractive formal study, probably at Wavertree. The year is probably 1937 for the engine, obviously fairly recently re-painted, has now received the new red shaded style of insignia, introduced in the second half of that year.

The 'Royal Scots'

The 'Royal Scots' were without doubt the archetypal LMS express passenger class, spanning as they did both the Fowler and Stanier eras. Introduced in parallel boiler form in 1927, without smoke deflectors and with standard Fowler tenders, they were rarely captured by Treacy's camera in this style, his record being almost entirely confined to their final thirty years or so from the mid-1930s until scrapping. He is on record as having stated that the rebuilt form (1943 onwards) was his favourite LMS type, but be they with parallel boiler or rebuilt, hardly a change of significance escaped his attention after 1934.

66

Almost as soon as the 'Scots' had received Stanier tenders, many of them were also fitted with modified smoke deflectors, but not always at the same time. This view at Standish Junction shows No.6115 Welsh Guardsman *displaying both modifications. It also carries the short lived 1936-7 style of sans-serif insignia. The train is southbound, the leading carriage, a through GWR brake composite, probably being destined for detachment at Crewe; all three principal periods of LMS carriage design are represented in the main train.*

By the start of the BR period, some two thirds of the engines had been rebuilt with taper boilers but those which remained in original condition had scarcely changed from their later 1930s configuration. No.46163 Civil Service Rifleman *was one such, not being rebuilt until 1953. It is seen here, c1949, on the southbound climb to Shap in a rather grubby early BR livery of black with LNWR style lining.*

67

(Opposite, above) In 1935, Stanier took the frames of an experimental high pressure 4-6-0 Fury and fitted them with a new taper boiler, thus producing, in effect, a very handsome taper boilered engine of 'Royal Scot' power potential. It was numbered 6170 and called British Legion. Eric Treacy photographed it regularly but not, as far as is known in its very original 1935 form with angled steam pipe covers between smokebox and cylinders. This view, at Edge Hill in 1936, shows its stylish lines to perfection, just after the straight steam pipe covers had been fitted.

(Opposite, below) British Legion became, in effect, the prototype for the rebuilds of the main class and from most angles of view was almost indistinguishable from them, its Stanier pattern cab with two side windows being the chief distinguishing point. It did not often venture much north of Lancashire, but in this view, the engine, still in 1946 LMS livery but now with BR markings, is seen leaving Preston for the north in 1948 with a very heavy train. The obvious lack of concern of the driver leaning out of the cab suggests a locomotive very much the master of its task.

The 'proper' rebuilds came into service during and after 1943 at a time when there was little if any glamour on the LMS system. They were painted unlined black and pretty soon became as dirty as the rest. This is well shown in this view of a 1944 rebuild, No.6120 Royal Inniskilling Fusilier photographed on Shap on 2nd May 1946 with at least fourteen bogies behind the tender en route from Euston to Perth. For once, Treacy gave us full details of the time and date. The war had been over for a year but the carriages are as dirty as the engine – a sadly all too common sight at these difficult times.

Things gradually improved during later 1946 and 1947, at least as far as cleanliness of the principal classes was concerned and the 'Royal Scots' mostly assumed the new lined black style which suited them well. They were worked virtually turn and turn about with the 4-6-2s, and were particularly common on the North Wales route. This is No.6112 Sherwood Forester, heading past Chester towards its home base at Holyhead with the 'down' 'Irish Mail'.

In BR days, smoke deflectors were universally fitted to the rebuilt 'Scots' but only one of them, No.6115 Scots Guardsman, assumed this guise during LMS days; for a couple of years or so it was the only example. The engine is in back gear with the blower on, having just set back onto the parcels train featured in the previous chapter. Treacy took the opportunity to produce this fine posed study, but also ensured that the LNWR 'furniture' in the form of ground and running signals give pictorial quality to an essentially record shot. The engine itself was the last rebuild to run in BR service and is preserved in the form shown here.

After the first two engines (Nos 6200-1) were built in 1933, the remaining ten, Nos 6203-12, did not appear until 1935 and were considerably modified as a result of development work with the first two. Most obviously, in purely visual terms, they displayed longer fireboxes, revised reversing gear rodding and more substantial motion bracket support. They were also fitted from new with standard Stanier 9 ton tenders. All these features are shown on this view of No. 6207 Princess Arthur of Connaught *on the 'down' 'Royal Scot' train ascending Shap in 1936.*

The 'Princess Royals'

The first class of Stanier 4-6-2, generally nicknamed "Lizzies" after the 1936 exploits of No.6201 *Princess Elizabeth*, actually appeared in 1933, but Treacy seems never to have photographed either of the two pioneer engines in their original configuration with flat sided tenders or even with the replacement standard 9 ton variety. This was just about his only omission; subsequent to 1935 there was little which went on in this group of engines which he failed to record. There were only twelve engines in the class proper and they displayed several detailed differences. This survey takes the story from c1935 to 1950. There were more changes to come after this time, including the fitting of domed boilers but the only deviation from the strict LMS configuration which I have allowed, solely in the interests of completeness, is a single view of the BR rebuild of No.46202 which started life in LMS days as the famous turbine driven 4-6-2. Its basic form was based on the 'Princess' type and it was a particular Treacy favourite during his Liverpool days.

After 1935, the next visible change to the "Lizzies" was to fit new pattern high sided 10 ton tenders. No.6201 Princess Elizabeth itself is seen here c1937/8 at Mossley Hill, shorly after receiving one. By now, the engine had also lost its record breaking domed boiler in favour of one of the original domeless type with prominent outside feed pipes leading up to the top feed clacks. There were, in LMS days, three boilers for the first two engines and until modifications were made in BR days, they would not fit any of the other members of the class. One of these three was the only domed "Lizzie" boiler in the LMS period but, search though I have, I cannot find a Treacy picture of it in service on either 6200 or 6201.

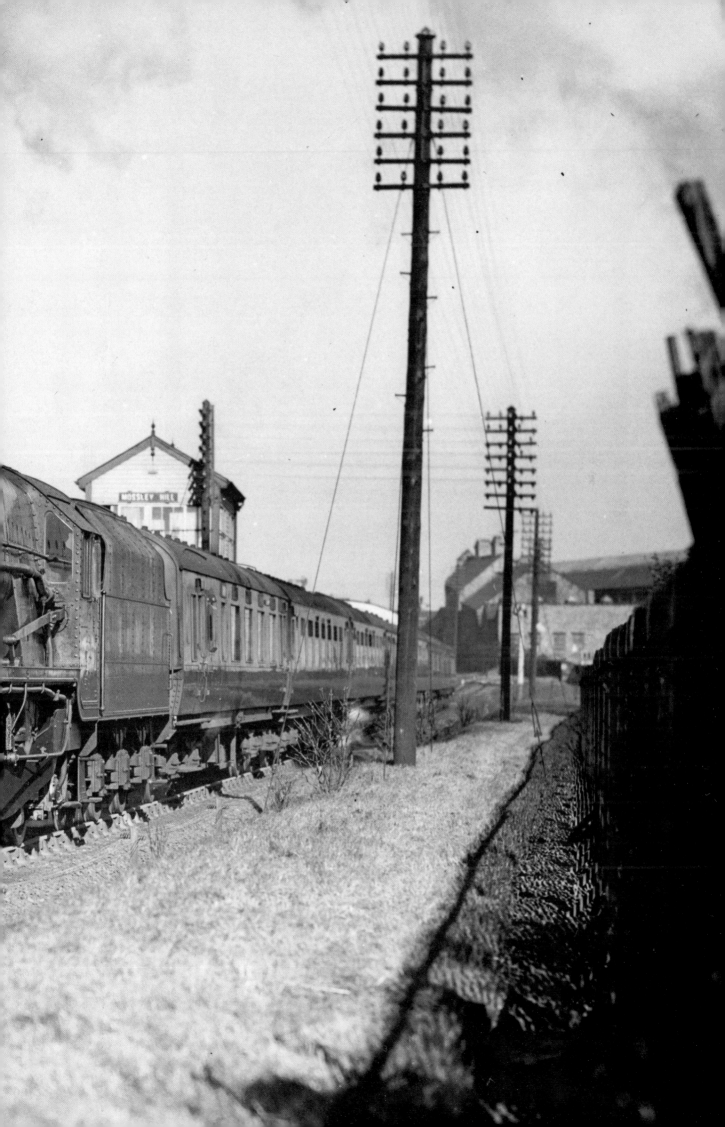

"Turbomotive'

Before considering the later variations of the 'Princesses' it would not be proper to omit No.6202 "Turbomotive", the unofficial nickname given to Stanier's one and only experimental locomotive. It was built in 1935, using the set of frames which had originally been intended for a third conventional 4-6-2 of the 6200/6201 type. In the event, Stanier was persuaded to try his great experiment and it caused considerable contemporary interest. It was also more than uncommonly handsome and the famous American designer Raymond Loewy described it as '. . . an outstanding example of the "British School" . . . one of the most beautiful pieces of machinery ever designed by man.' Treacy liked it too!

'Turbo' was a considerable success but, being unique, cost rather more to operate than a standard "Lizzie" even though fully up to standard as regards performance. It was, therefore, rebuilt in 1952 to conventional form, becoming in effect a sort of cross breed between the original 'Princess' type and the later 'Coronation' class. Named *Princess Anne*, it was, in effect, the very last LMS steam locomotive design, owing nothing to the BR standards which had already begun to appear. Sadly, No.46202 was written off after the disastrous Harrow double collision in October 1952, having only run a few thousand miles in its new form.

Treacy's images of No.6202 around Liverpool are very familiar and although this view at Wavertree has been seen before, I have only ever seen it reproduced with the signals partly cropped away. I therefore felt readers might like to see the whole picture, it is one of Treacy's best.

(Opposite, above) This considerably less well known Treacy view of No.6202 shows the left hand side of the engine as it accelerates through Mossley Hill with the 'up' 'Merseyside Express'. The much longer turbine casing on this side of the locomotive compared with that shown in the previous picture, housed the forward turbine; the shorter casing housed the reverse turbine.

(Opposite, below) The view here shows Princess Anne at Edge Hill shed in September 1952. The slight change in footplate level caused by the adoption of the 'Duchess' type front end was visually somewhat unfortunate. Whether original or rebuilt, No.46202 was the only LMS 4-6-2 never to trail a high sided 10 ton tender.

This view of No.6203 Princess Margaret Rose *at Wavert*
Junction with its new tender in 1937 makes an interest
comparison with the picture of No.6201 on page 72, for the an
of view is much the same. The longer firebox of the 6203-12 ser
is not readily apparent, save by close examination, but
recessed steam pipes to the top feed clacks are a point
difference. Note the more substantial motion bracket compar
with that of No.6201.

The 'Princess Royals' became something of a fixture on
Liverpool trains during the later 1930s so it is not surprising t
Treacy saw most if not all of them. This is the last of the cla
No.6212, now fitted with a smokebox door with 'dog' t
fastenings – something of a retrograde step one feels whose eff
does not seem to have been recorded for posterity. The engine v
somewhat confusingly named Duchess of Kent *and is se*
making a spectacular, albeit highly inefficient smoke effect a.
passes through Edge Hill on its way to London with the '
'Merseyside Express'. By all accounts, the dramatic smo
effects visible on many Treacy pictures were not always m
coincidence! The leading two carriages are also interesting, be
dating from the mildly experimental 1930-32 period when
LMS was moving from wooden to steel panelled stock. At
front is one of a small but luxurious series of wooden bodied bra
composites built in 1930 and subsequently rebuilt with Star
type panelling while behind it is an 'all steel' brake third from
year or two later. Altogether it is a most interesting picture a
typical of the detail which can be seen in Treacy's work.

It is believed that all the 'Princess Royals' went straight from LMS crimson to the post-war 1946 livery without an intervening utility black phase and here is proof in the case of No.6205 *Princess Victoria. The engine is still clearly red but the cabside numbers are in the 'high up' 1946 and later position. It may even have reached BR in this form since this picture, at Edge Hill No.2 Box is believed to date from 1947. Note also the unique motion bracket support on this member of the class. This was fitted to enable the inside valves to derive their motion from the outside valve gear, thus saving two sets of Walschaerts motion. A rather neater solution to achieve the same effect was used on the next series of 4-6-2s, the 'Coronation' class.*

This second view of Princess Victoria, *now as BR No.46205 and painted black with LNWR lining c1948, gives a clearer view of the unique motion support fitted to this engine. The location is, Shap and the train may well be a Euston-Perth express. If so, the engine is likely to be working right through from its home base, Crewe.*

77

No.M6206 Princess Marie Louise, *was probably the only LMS 4-6-2 to get this short-lived form of BR numbering, early in 1948 before the addition of 40000 to the old LMS numbers was settled. It was still in 1946 LMS livery at Thrimby on the southbound ascent to Shap, heading back to its home depot at Crewe. The engine was also unique in one other respect, being the only 'Princess' to be fitted with a 10 ton tender which also had a steam operated 'coal pusher' at the back of the coal space. This was an experiment, later adopted universally with the 'Coronation' class.*

(Opposite, above) No.46210 Lady Patricia *climbing Camden Bank in 1948. The only non-LMS feature is the number itself but even the front numberplate has LMS type figures rather than the later BR sans-serif form. This view shows the most common configuration of the 'Princess Royals' at the end of the LMS period. Even in 1948, three of the first four carriages are of LNWR origin.*

(Opposite, below) This fine study of Duchess of Kent *again, now as No.46212 with proper smokebox door and in BR experimental lined black livery, concludes Treacy's record, for the time being, of these famous engines during their LMS period. It is seen climbing to Shap with the 'up' 'Mid-Day Scot', c1948.*

Treacy's photographic record of the first five blue streamliners on the 'Coronation Scot' train is formidable and several quite majestic examples appear both in this book and elsewhere. By contrast, this is a somewhat everyday picture of No.6223 Princess Alice climbing Shap Bank but it has its own interest. Firstly, the engine seems rather grimy and the deposit of soot on the casing in front of the chimney may even hint that the streamlining was not always effective. The exhaust is, however, pretty clean and not too prominent and the driver is obviously quite unconcerned, both facts being indicative of efficiency. This sort of view was probably far more typical of this working than the more spectacular shots.

The 'Coronations'

The 'Princess Coronation' class 4-6-2s, to give them their full official nomenclature, emerged in 1937 in streamlined form as a development of the 'Princess Royal' type for high speed heavy haulage duties. They were, in all vital respects, a considerable improvement over Stanier's first Pacifics and by general consent are regarded as his finest achievement, many neutral observers also rating them as Britain's finest express passenger locomotives from any source. They were justly famous and much has been written of them. Treacy saw them all from birth to scrapping and his photographic record must be without parallel. In this survey, the story is taken to less than the half-way point in their lives. The oldest of them was only eleven years old at Nationalisation, at which point they still had another sixteen years to go.

In later years, the class became collectively known by the unofficial designation 'Duchess', inspired by the naming policy adopted for ten of the first fifteen examples. In some ways this was a more appropriate title since it clearly hinted at their dignified and majestic nature. The enginemen simply called them "Big Lizzies", in truth, that is just what they were!

In 1938, five more streamliners (Nos 6225-9) were added to the total, this time painted Midland Red with gold stripes, thereafter the standard colour for the streamliners. They were the first with 'Duchess' names, they went into general service and Treacy managed to photograph them rather more often than most. This is No.6227 Duchess of Devonshire, none too clean again, passing Edge Hill with the usual mixture of different styles of carriages representing all three LMS design periods. At this time, the LMS was making a conscious attempt to keep the blue engines reserved for the 'Coronation Scot'; in consequence, the red ones tended to get used for anything appropriate. In these circumstances, the streamlining and special livery almost seemed something of a wasted effort!

(Above) The somewhat inappropriate visual combination of a new streamlined engine and a complete rag bag of carriages is even more marked in this 1939 view of the brand new No.6235 City of Birmingham passing through Edge Hill at a point only some four or five carriage lengths further down the line than the previous picture. The train is from Liverpool to the West of England and the first carriage is an ex-LNWR brake composite (built for the Central Wales services), followed by a through GWR carriage and at least three pre-Stanier LMS vehicles. The engine is depicted at almost the same angle as Duchess of Devonshire and the slightly longer casing of the new style double chimney can just be distinguished. No.6235 was the first 'Coronation' to be given a double chimney from new and also the first to carry a 'City' theme name. Like all the red streamliners, it never had cylinder relief valves and this very clear picture shows how the casing was modified below the cylinders (see picture, page 80). Other interesting aspects of the streamliners revealed here are their special 'winged' headlamps and their lack of depot identification plate. No.6235 was a Camden engine at this time and probably came off this at Crewe.

(Below) It is absolutely certain that William Stanier did not favour streamlining and between the building of Nos 6229 and 6235, five more 'Duchesses' came out non-streamlined in 1938. They revealed an outline which eventually characterised the whole class and, again, Treacy captured them all on film. This is one of his unknown views, No.6233 Duchess of Sutherland climbing Shap and, judging from the nearly vertical direction of the exhaust from its single chimney, making quite a fuss of it. It was the last example of this series, No.6234 Duchess of Abercorn, which was put on test in 1939 with and without a double chimney, eventually leading to the fitting of double chimneys as standard. No.6233 is preserved much as shown here but with the double chimney modification.

82

Wartime railway pictures by any amateur photographer were rare, but Treacy did manage a few. This view shows a dishevelled Princess Alice, still blue (more or less!) but now with double chimney, tackling Shap with a typically heavy wartime Euston-Glasgow formation of at least 15 bogies. There is no sign of a dining car and the leading carriage is one of the 1926 'all steel' open thirds, ordered by the LMS to assist the steel industry at the time. Treacy records this picture as 1942 but the next picture suggests that it might have been two or three years later.

This picture looks suspiciously like the same working as the previous one and at much the same location, but the engine, No.6249 City of Sheffield, was not built until 1944. It was one of a small wartime batch, ordered as streamliners but turned out in non-streamlined form. They did, however, receive streamlined pattern tenders which were already built. This picture shows such a tender, by now devoid of its rearward extensions but still retaining its lower fairings. The engine was painted utility unlined black and was filthy, the date being no later than 1945.

(Opposite) After the war, starting in 1945, the streamlined 'Coronations' had their casings removed and the few new examples were built with a slightly more utilitarian front end. They were also fitted with the smoke deflectors which experience had shown to be necessary on a non-streamlined engine with a double chimney and consequential softer exhaust. These features are all shown in these views of the then fairly new No.6254 City of Stoke on Trent based at Camden but seen here in the new standard 1946 express livery at Edge Hill. Treacy analysed this particular engine quite closely and took some evocative detailed close-ups, one of which, a three-quarter rear view, is also shown here. It is not the better known view which features a group of railway enthusiasts looking at the engine; this one shows the crew!

City of Birmingham was the first 'Coronation' to be built with a double chimney and also the first to be de-streamlined (in 1945). Treacy not only photographed it when new (page 82) but also at every subsequent stage. This splendid view on Shap Bank dates from 1948 when the engine was in LMS 1946 livery but with BR number, 46235. The ugly sloping smokebox consequent upon de-streamlining is very prominent and this aspect led to contemporary enthusiasts calling them 'semi-streamlined' ('semi' for short – ugh!).

In later BR days, fully circular smokeboxes were fitted to all ex-streamliners and in this final form, No.46235 is now preserved at the Birmingham Museum. It was in fact, the officially selected example for preservation although two more also survive from the 'Duchess' series. The train itself, in a mixture of LMS and BR livery is described by Treacy as the 'down' 'Royal Scot' and is certainly composed mostly of Stanier stock, as would be expected at this time. But there is an LNWR carriage second from the engine and a twelve-wheel diner at vehicle number six, neither of which would normally be expected in this particular train.

The last purely LMS Pacific was No.6256 Sir William A. Stanier F.R.S. built right at the end of 1947. Very soon afterwards, it was modified to accept electric lighting and paradoxically, it was not until quite late in BR days that the engine resumed its original LMS appearance. As far as can be judged, Treacy did not catch it in original guise until it had reverted back – by which time it had also assumed the BR version of the LMS red livery. This picture is therefore, somewhat misleading since, although it shows the original LMS form of the engine, it actually dates from 1964! The view also indicates the cabside and trailing truck modifications given to this 'ultimate' LMS engine, features which it shared with its BR built 'twin' No.46257 City of Salford.

The '5XPs'

The largest single collection of LMS express passenger engines was a group of 263 4-6-0 locomotives which became collectively known as the '5XPs', but before considering Treacy's coverage of this group, it might be helpful to look at the actual '5XP' term itself, mainly for the benefit of those whose memory does not go back before c1951. In 1923, the LMS classified its locomotives into power groups, based on the old Midland system dating back to 1907. By the 1930s, these ran from Class 0 (smallest) to Class 7 (most powerful). The 'Royal Scots' were the first to be put into Class 6, prior to which, Class 5 was the highest category – given to a few pre-Group types which were more powerful than the biggest Midland engines which were never more than Class 4. In 1933, the more powerful 4-6-2s naturally fell into Class 7, but there was already a joker in the pack, originating from about the time of introduction of the 'Royal Scots'. This arose from the re-building with larger boilers of some of the four cylinder ex-LNWR 'Sir Gilbert Claughton' class 4-6-0 engines. At the Grouping, the LMS had assigned Power Class 5 to this series, but the larger boilered rebuilds were in an intermediate category, not quite Class 6 but rather better than Class 5. They were, accordingly, designated Class 5X – a sort of superior Class 5 if you like. The 'P' suffix arrived in 1928 in consequence of the LMS deciding to differentiate between Freight (F) and Passenger (P) types.

In due course, the LMS developed this '5X' type in two stages, first by putting the new boiler on a three cylinder chassis and later by replacing the parallel boiler on the three cylinder version with Stanier's tapered variety. What makes matters more confusing is that the three main groups of engines within this classification also had class names. The original ex-LNWR rebuilds were still known as 'Claughtons' (logical enough), the next generation was referred to officially as the 'Patriot' class (unofficially and more accurately known as "Baby Scots") while the third, taper boiler development eventually became known as 'Jubilees' because of a naming policy adopted over a year after many of them came into service.

Of course, logic would have caused the classification to run from Class 0 to Class 8, making the 'Royal Scots' Class 7, the 4-6-2s Class 8 and the new intermediate sized 4-6-0s Class 6. This indeed took place during BR days but in LMS times, these medium sized 4-6-0s were always '5XPs' and this term took firm root. In fact, most railwaymen could not even be bothered with the 'P', so '5X' became the common nomenclature, even after BR sorted the whole business out by making them Class 6!

(Opposite) During the first few years of BR, more or less coinciding with the pre-standard period (during which time the railway was still basically LMS apart from new colour schemes), the Stanier 4-6-2s were given a new but rather short-lived blue livery of somewhat Caledonian Railway aspect. By no means all of them received it but, in my view, it was the best colour scheme which BR ever used on the 4-6-2s until LMS crimson was re-instated in 1957. We therefore take our leave of the LMS 'Coronations', for the time being, with this magnificent 1950 study of No.46255 City of Hereford, *seen departing from the north end of Shrewsbury Station wearing the new blue livery. This final LMS configuration was the external form in which a later generation was to get to know the 'Duchesses', so it seems a quite appropriate point at which to conclude this particular survey.*

(Overleaf) The original 'Patriots' changed their appearance but little, save for liveries, until either scrapped or rebuilt and during later LMS and BR days tended not to be quite so much in the limelight as had been the case during the early 1930s. This is a typical 1948 task – a 'down' relief at the top of Camden Bank headed by No.45515 Caernarvon. *The engine, based at Preston, is in LMS 1946 livery with BR markings and the train probably bound for Blackpool. It is entirely in LMS colours and represents the usual 'ad hoc' mixture of types from LNWR to Stanier vintage.*

These views, taken at almost precisely the same angle, clearly illustrate the gestation of the '5XP' type. No. 6004, the last survivor of the class, was a reboilered four cylinder 'Claughton', formerly Prince Louise, while No.5508, one of the few un-named examples, depicts the original parallel boilered 'Patriot' type utilising the same boiler but now fitted to a three cylinder chassis of 'Royal Scot' type. The reason for the "Baby Scot" soubriquet obvious, although the LMS preferred the 'Patriot' designation, derived from the name eventually given to the first member No.5500.

No.6004 was based at Willesden at the time, probably 1946-7. It is still painted red and carries the headcode of a fully fitted freight train, probably destined for London – a common sort of working for this engine in its final years. No.5508 is similarly occupied, this time on an express freight and in 1946 livery. In both cases, the trains contain a very high proportion of covered vans – see also Chapter 7.

After the success of the rebuilt 'Royal Scots', the LMS next embarked on a similar rebuilding programme for the 'Patriots', the next oldest of the three cylinder 4-6-0s and also with parallel boilers. The process began in 1946 and went on into 1949 but was brought to a halt with only 18 engines converted. It seems likely that, but for Nationalisation, the whole class would have been converted. This 1948 view at Chester of the 'up' 'Irish Mail' shows one of the earlier rebuilds, dating from 1947 and still in LMS livery, renumbered 45514. Named Holyhead, it was, by coincidence, also shedded there. The leading van (see page 63, lower) – is again a post-war rebuild but the first class brake behind it is quite unique and can be positively identified as No.5010, built in 1932 as the only steel panelled example of a small group of luxury brakes introduced in 1929. It was actually built as a 'one-off' replacement for the original wooden bodied example, damaged beyond repair in the Leighton Buzzard accident.

So much for basic history, of which much more could be and has been said; most of it need not concern us here, save to remark that a pair of 'Jubilees' (in 1942) and a handful of 'Patriots' (1946-9) were further modified and given the 'Rebuilt Royal Scot' boiler, thus becoming for all practical purposes identical to the engines of the rebuilt 'Royal Scot' class. They were, without doubt, a more than confusing group of engines.

Treacy began to take pictures of the '5Xs' in the mid-1930s and, it has to be said, his record is not totally comprehensive. He did photograph both the reboilered 'Claughtons' and the original 'Patriots' but his most comprehensive coverage was of the final Stanier taper boilered variants, the 'Jubilees' and, later, the Class 6 rebuilds. The original Class 5XP 'Jubilees' were by far the most numerous (191 out of the total – 189 after two were rebuilt), followed by 52 'Patriots' (original and/or rebuilds) and no more than 20 reboilered 'Claughtons'. The original 'Jubilees' were also the most long-lived, so it is not too surprising that this next section is heavily biased in their favour; but we start by a brief look at the earlier designs.

Like all but one of the converted 'Scots', the rebuilt 'Patriots' came into service without smoke deflectors – BR fitted them later – but whereas the 'Scots' kept their original cabs, the 'Patriots' were given new Stanier style cabs, making them slightly more modern looking. This apart, the two types of rebuild were all but identical. Newly rebuilt in 1948, No.45535 Sir Herbert Walker K.C.B. is shown here at its home base Crewe. Like many former LMS express engines at this time, it was given LNWR style lined black livery, later to be adopted for mixed traffic types.

In 1934, Stanier put a taper boiler onto the "Baby Scot" chassis and thus started the building of the largest single group of LMS express engines, save for the Midland/LMS Compounds. The new '5XPs' were built to the tune of 191 examples between 1934 and 1936. Naming did not commence until 1935 when No.5642 exchanged numbers with the first of the series, No.5552 and was named Silver Jubilee. Thereafter, most enthusiasts called them 'Jubilees'; the enginemen stuck to "Taper 5X" or even "red ones" so as to distinguish them from the contemporary

"black" Class 5 4-6-0s. This first view shows one of the original domeless engines, No.5576, built by the North British Locomotive Company in 1934, some time after 1937 when it became Bombay. The dome shaped feature on the boiler top was actually a top feed casing. The location is Clifton and Lowther, heading south with a train consisting of all three design periods of LMS stock ('all steel' third brake of 1931 leading) and an LNWR full brake bringing up the the rear. There appears to be no dining provision.

This domeless 'Jubilee' No.5635 Tobago, *received its name in 1936 and is seen here at Wavertree very soon afterwards, clearly fairly fresh off shops and carrying the short-lived 1936 style sans-serif insignia which many of the class received at first re-paint. No.5635 was one of the second batch of 1934 Crewe built engines which received shorter chimneys than the contemporary North British series.*

Later 'Jubilees' were built from new with domed boilers and separate top feed. They also had somewhat longer fireboxes – a point not always easy to spot. This is No.5692 Cyclops *at its home base Preston in 1936, the year of its building. It carries the older style 1928-36 insignia, gold with black shading and the engine was named from the outset. A fairly easy way of 'spotting' a long-firebox 'Jubilee' was to note the two prominent hemispherical cover plates on the shoulder of the firebox between top and sides. There were other differences too, of course.*

This picture also shows an engine fitted with one of the far less common Stanier 3,500 gallon tenders – almost impossible to distinguish from the normal riveted 4,000 gallon version unless the view was such as to enable the shorter wheelbase to be identified. The flush sided Stanier tenders were always of the 4,000 gallon type.

The final new 'Jubilees' coincided with the new 1936 style insignia, being outshopped from new in this style. They were readily identified by their new style front numberplates, well seen here on No.5734 Meteor on the 'up' fast line approaching Whitmore. Note the reversion to taller chimney.

This view of Carlisle-based No.5688 Polyphemus, heading south through Penrith, probably in 1938, shows another long-firebox 'Jubilee', this time repainted with the red shaded insignia of the traditional scroll/serif type, introduced in late 1937 after the abandonment of the 1936 pattern. The visible portion of the train consists wholly of former LNWR stock. The leading brake is a turn-of-century six wheeler while the passenger vehicles are 'Toplight' corridors of World War I vintage.

In time, changes began to take place within the class, most visible being the 1936 tender exchange with the 'Royal Scots'. In consequence, seventy 'Jubilees' received Fowler 3,500 gallon tenders and mostly kept them for the rest of their lives. They were chosen from those engines which had originally received 4,000 gallon Stanier tenders.

A further change to the engines themselves was to fit the former domeless engines with domed boilers and separate top feed; they were, in fact, the same boilers rebuilt. Both alterations are seen here in this classic Treacy study of No.5603 Solomon Islands, *climbing through the cuttings between Lime Street and Edge Hill. The date is probably c1945-6 for although the engine is still red (just!), the cabside numerals are in the 'high-up' position adopted by the LMS towards the end of the war.*

This near identical view to the previous shot (taken the same day?) shows another tender variation in what was undoubtedly a confusing class in this respect. No.5613 Kenya was one of only ten 'Jubilees' to receive a particularly ugly form of flat sided 3,500 gallon tender, just visible in this view. The engine itself has received the same boiler modifications as had No.5603 and also carries its cabside number in the 'high' position, this time with plain black livery.

Very many 'Jubilees', probably the majority, succumbed to plain black livery during the war years. This is No.5734 again, still carrying its 1936 numberplate but now in standard LMS wartime 'utility' finish with cabside numerals aligned with the tender lettering. The location is the 'down' fast line at Bourne End, c1946.

The fitting of replacement Fowler tenders to the 'Jubilees' was a somewhat random business, examples of all the locomotive variants being involved. This is one of the final long firebox series with tall chimney, No.5716 *Swiftsure*, leaving its home base at Carlisle in 1947 with an unidentified northbound express. It is painted in full 1946 livery and still carries its 1936 pattern numberplate.

Before leaving the LMS period, I thought it would be quite amusing to see if Treacy had recorded the preserved 'Jubilees' during their working years. This is in fact a 'joker' for it shows No.5742 Connaught, *the very last of the series, carrying the experimental double chimney boiler now fitted to the preserved No.5596* Bahamas! *This boiler moved around quite a bit as engines went through shops and did not arrive on*

Bahamas *until BR days. The fact that the experiment was not more widespread suggests that it was not altogether successful. However, No.5742 carried this boiler for quite a while and this view, dating from c1946-7, shows the engine, at the time based at Bushbury, leaving Euston with a Wolverhampton express, the locomotive itself being in utility unlined black.*

Treacy's contemporary record of the other preserved engines is rather better. Here is No.5593 Kolhapur in 1947, in much the same physical configuration as now preserved (save for the 1946 livery carried here), storming past Camden under the Regent's Park Road bridge with a 'down' express for Manchester, at the time its home base. A later generation was to know it as one of the final few at Leeds (Holbeck) and it is now, of course, based at Tyseley. This engine was one of the original North British domeless series and received its domed boiler c1936.

(Opposite, above) Eric Treacy also captured No.5690 Leander at much the same time and place, this time Euston Station itself. This engine was one of several 'Jubilees' which managed to survive the war in red livery. In those days, engines were not repainted unless strictly necessary and Leander seems to have fared better than most; the paintwork does not seem too bad and is by no means as dirty as some. The engine has obviously received some partial attention to the paintwork on the cabside, for although there are traces of pre-war lining, the number itself is in the post-war position.

For about ten years between c1941 (the onset of wartime utility painting) and 1951 (ie about the time when most of them were standard BR green), the 'Jubilees' presented a pretty inconsistent appearance in terms of livery. This survey concludes with two early BR examples. The first (opposite, below) shows No.45681 Aboukir, a long firebox engine, leaving its home town Liverpool. The engine appears to be unlined black but the tender carries LMS 1946 livery with BR markings. The second view (above) shows one of the original 1934 North British domeless engines, No.45565 Victoria, now fitted with a dome and painted in experimental BR apple green with LNWR lining, passing Marley Junction, near Keighley, with a 'down' Edinburgh express in 1948.

Chapter 5

Traffic and Trains I
Express Passenger

The express passenger train has been and always will be the most publicly known and most prestigious operation of the railways of Britain. No matter that in LMS days the Company made a good deal more money by hauling freight, expresses were almost always the operations which received most publicity and were equally regularly the first recipients of new locomotives and rolling stock. Because of Treacy's liking for this form of operation, his record of LMS express steam trains has now become one of the most vivid encapsulations of the then current 'state of the art' which we have available to us.

As with most of his works, Treacy did not venture into every highway and byway which express working could encompass, but since most of his activity was carried out on the main lines of the most 'express-conscious' of the LMS constituents – the LNWR and Midland – we do have a very comprehensive picture available. Yet again, of course, the intention behind the pictures was not overtly historical and one has to do a bit of digging to get the best out of them, but the effort is well worthwhile.

Happily for posterity, Treacy's record of express trains is not confined to the principal and most obvious workings, many of which have been included in the previous chapter. He also recorded a fair number of lesser operations which carried the mandatory headlamps over each buffer and some of these are given prominence here. They remind us of much which is now forgotten and a few words in amplification will not come amiss.

Firstly, a steam hauled express was thus categorised solely in terms of its omission of intermediate stops. It did not have to fulfil any mandatory conditions with regard to length, type of carriage or class of locomotive and in consequence, it could vary from a massive assemblage of corridor coaches including dining and sleeping cars to an almost improper assortment of but a handful of vehicles. It did not have to have corridor stock, its locomotive could be anything within reason as long as it had a vacuum brake capable of satisfying the mandatory 'fail-safe' rules of automatic braking, it did not have to carry a name and there was nothing at all to say how fast it had to go!

Supervening this overall blanket definition, there was no great effort, at least as far as the LMS was concerned, to make up what might be called 'tidy' formations. It is a constant source of frustration to the writer that, try as he will, he cannot convince a newer generation, brought up on a gruel-thin diet of standardised BR MkI stock and mono-stylistic HST formations, that in steam days on the LMS, or other railways for that matter, it was extremely rare to find a complete set of homogeneously styled carriages in any one formation. This is of particular relevance in

(Opposite) We start with yet another look at the 'down' 'Mid-Day Scot' at Kilburn High Road, c1937 – see also Chapter 3 – but this time properly identified by the weekday reporting number on the smokebox front of 'Princess' Pacific No.6210 Lady Patricia. *Unbelievably, Treacy has captured yet another variation of those first three carriages. This time the leading brake third is 'inside out' so to speak.*

(Opposite) Rounding the bend at Treacy's favourite Kilburn High Road location, also c1937, 'Royal Scot' No.6147 The Northamptonshire Regiment, *does not seem to be having too much trouble with an unidentified down express. The coach formation is typical of much LMS Western Division (ie ex-LNWR area) practice at that time. A 1930 wooden bodied brake composite leads followed by a steel panelled open third of 1931. Next comes one of the original Stanier 1933 third class twelve wheel diners followed by a slightly later open composite diner (without kitchen) and an early Stanier corridor third. The rest is unclear but seems mostly third class, indicative of the rather low proportion of first class on most LMS express trains.*

the field of modelmaking which, increasingly as years go by, is probably the only practical way of re-creating many of the more subtle nuances of the by-gone scene. True, the LMS built hundreds of flush-sided Stanier coaches as it had, previously, built hundreds of the fully panelled variety but, as Treacy's pictures more than adequately reveal, a full set of one style was very much the exception. Perhaps it does not matter save to the ultra-pedantic, but it does rather suggest that we could, with advantage, examine more closely the evidence provided by photographers of the scene.

Treacy's pictures provide this evidence, largely because their quality is such as to allow the sort of detailed examination of the subject matter in a way which, I am sure, was furthest from his mind at the time he opened his camera shutter. Thus, while not wishing in any way to minimise the artistic quality of his work, I hope it will be understood why, in this section of the book, the

Stanier's first locomotive design for the LMS was a taper boilered version of the more well known Hughes/Fowler 'Horwich' 2-6-0s. Only 40 were built and were mostly used for freight but Treacy has caught one, No.42961, on passenger duty at Chester in 1948 with a secondary express bound for Birkenhead, its home base. Although a typically attractive and perfectly composed Treacy 'picture', it contains a wealth of historical detail apart from the self-evident LNWR setting. The crisp detail of the engine itself shows some of the features which made this class different from most subsequent Stanier types. Of these, one might mention the horizontal and rather low set cylinders (most Stanier engines had cylinders tucked well under the running plate at about a 5° angle), the distinctive top-feed and the pure 'Horwich' cab, the latter copied from the earlier 2-6-0s and clearly the main design influence on the subsequent Stanier cab. The first three vehicles of the train consist of a former GWR 'Siphon' van, a nearly forty year old LNWR corridor third and a much newer Stanier composite.

The 'Royal Scots' were not only used on principal long distance workings and space starved modelmakers may well find inspiration in this attractive view. No.6149 The Middlesex Regiment, is seen passing Milepost 185 on the West Coast Main Line near Warrington, c1938, hauling a nice little five coach express including an ex-MR horsebox and an ex-LNWR full brake. The passenger vehicles form a three coach 'Inter-Corridor Set' of wood panelled LMS standard stock of the 1920s, formed up brake third, composite, brake third. The LMS used many such sets from a whole range of pre and post-Group design periods; there was a four coach version too which would either have had two composites or an extra full third.

caption details tend rather to concentrate on the minutiae. This also explains the inclusion in this section of rather more than normal the number of previously published views, although I hope not to excess. The fact is that they can tell us much more than they have done so far and it is my hope that this section will help to indicate how.

The pictures are grouped more or less geographically, they are a genuinely random selection in terms of subject matter and I have tried to balance the more obvious examples with a good leavening of the lesser known operations. I have also, in one case, 'The Thames-Clyde Express', deliberately tried to extract every single ounce of evidence which Treacy gives us of the way in which but one train changed its nature over quite a short period of time. As always, matters of peripheral interest to the main subject of this chapter will also be included where they add to the interpretive nature of the picture.

This view at Standish is revealed as being a year or two earlier than the previous picture by virtue of the older pattern smoke deflectors and the black shaded insignia on No.6101 *Royal Scots Grey* and was probably taken shortly after the fitting of the replacement Stanier tender in 1936. The train is fascinating, albeit unidentified. The first four vehicles (a through portion?) consist of a 1903 MR clerestory brake composite, two Stanier corridor thirds, the leading one quite new (simple livery), the next being of 1933 vintage (shallow window ventilators, full livery) and an-LNWR full brake. Behind this is another of the 1930 composite brakes (page 100, lower) which seems to have had its projecting lookout removed, a twelve-wheel diner, two more Stanier eight-wheelers and what looks suspiciously like a six-wheel full brake. The last two identifiable vehicles are another Stanier corridor and a pre-1930 wooden panelled coach. Only the sheer clarity of Treacy's technique permits such detailed examination yet, overall, it was obviously taken purely as a picture.

The illustration on page 50 in Chapter 3 showed some milk traffic on a 'Royal Scot' hauled express leaving Penrith. This and the next two pictures continue the story, quite a complicated one if truth be told. This view, at Clifton and Lowther is the only one of the whole group which Treacy records with any accuracy, stating it to be an 'up' express from Perth and Aberdeen. Almost certainly it is the same working. The engine is No.6109 Royal Engineer, carrying the 1936 style of LMS insignia and still with angled top smoke deflectors, while the date can be no later than mid-1937. The shed plate is indistinct but has a single figure number, probably Crewe.

The milk is still contained in a road tank mounted on a flat wagon and the passenger formation, this time entirely Stanier corridor stock, is almost the same and can be precisely specified from this very clear view: Full brake, third, third kitchen/diner, composite non-kitchen diner, third, composite, composite, brake third. After this comes a wonderful assortment of non-passenger coaching stock: LNWR bogie brake, Midland six wheel parcels van, Midland/LMS six-wheel fish van and a vacuum fitted cattle wagon, the latter presumably empty!

(Opposite, above) Back to Penrith again but now no earlier than mid-1937. The engine, No.6138 The London Irish Rifleman, now carries new red shaded 1937 style characters and the freight wagons on the left indicate that the new 1937 style of wagon marking (small lettering in the lower left corner) has just begun to appear. Is it the same train again? Well, this time the engine is from Carlisle whereas previously it was not and the train is rather more untidy in its formation, as far as can be seen. However, the milk traffic is still there; there is again a non-passenger vehicle behind the tender – cf page 50 – and the main train leads off with a full brake, so it is very similar in character. That the milk is now carried in six-wheel rail tank wagons probably reflects the fact that 1937 was the first year when the use of six wheels became normal and, indeed, mandatory on purpose built vehicles. Prior to this, four wheel milk tanks had been built and used but since six wheels were regarded as more stable at high speed for this traffic, there was a short-lived compromise period with road tanks on six wheel rail chassis, during which time the old four wheel rail tanks themselves were converted to six wheel form. Treacy recorded it!

(Opposite, below) The story is completed as far as it can be in this more revealing picture at Euxton Junction, c1937/8, again with a Carlisle engine, this time No.6136 The Border Regiment, heading south with what is almost certainly the same working. This time the six-wheel milk tanks lead off which, with the livery/configuration of the engine (note new type smoke deflectors), again help to date the picture no earlier than 1937. The LNWR full brake is followed by a set of carriages whose formation, although a bit more ragged, is not unlike that shown at Clifton and Lowther a year earlier, all of which suggests that it really was the same train in all cases.

The presence of older stock both between the leading Stanier carriage and the twelve-wheel dining car and elsewhere, suggests some temporary strengthening, possibly indicating a different time of year or maybe even a Saturday only version of the train. There is, for example, rather less in the way of non-passenger stock at the rear, a solitary horsebox in fact. Any or all of this could quite easily explain the use of a Carlisle engine, rather than the Crewe based examples of the first two pictures. Would that Treacy had told us more, but then if he had been interested in this sort of detail, maybe the pictorial value would have suffered.

As it is, we are left with an astonishingly detailed record of these things and whatever the precise explanation of this particular group of pictures, their quality makes the detective work fascinating.

(Opposite, above) This four-coach train leaving Preston under express headlamps behind Bury based Stanier 2-6-4T No.2439 is almost certainly a semi-fast commuter service to the Manchester area. The period is again c1937-8 and the train itself is formed from two pairs of LMS standard 'Inter-District' lavatory non-corridor carriages, brake third and composite. These slightly superior non-corridors were built in the late 1920s for just this sort of operation but were not always seen quite so tidily used! A somewhat puzzling aspect is the 'LBL' branding clearly visible on the end of the first carriage. This was a former LYR term, copied by the LMS and used to designate sets of vehicles allocated to the Leeds/**B**radford/**L**iverpool services. What it was doing at Preston cannot be explained – perhaps a reader can help.

(Opposite, below) Treacy's record amply reveals the extent to which the LMS West Coast route relied on 'Royal Scot' haulage for the vast bulk of express working in the mid-1930s. In this view on Shap, No.6140 The King's Royal Rifle Corps, a Preston engine, was probably in charge of the Keswick portion of the 'Lakes Express', the main train having gone to Windermere from Oxenholme. If so, the engine may have worked the whole train as far as Oxenholme and would come off the train at Penrith. The date must be later than 1936, the year the engine received its Stanier tender and was renamed from Hector. The train formation is brake third, third, brake composite and third, yet again revealing the low proportion of first class accommodation; even such as was provided was in the oldest carriage in the train.

Treacy took many magnificent views of 'Duchesses' on Shap Bank but this is one of his best, not seen for more than thirty years. It shows No.46233 Duchess of Sutherland recovering from what Treacy describes as a 'cruel check' just below Scout Green. The year is 1948 and the engine now has a double chimney and smoke deflectors. The train, which cannot positively be identified, is predominantly Stanier stock, perhaps the most interesting feature being a pair of the 1937 built articulated open carriages behind the twelve wheel diner (fourth vehicle). The engine carries a Crewe North shed plate and was working through to Scotland, Glasgow or Perth being, no doubt, its destination.

(Opposite) The double headed combination of Class 2P 4-4-0 and 'Jubilee' 4-6-0 was, if anything, more characteristic of the Midland than the West Coast Main Line, but these views show two such combinations at Shap and Penrith respectively, both dating from the mid-1940s. The MR style 4-4-0s are of two types, No.356 being genuinely ex-Midland (7ft wheels, RH drive) and No.652 the LMS standard continuation (6ft 9in wheels, LH drive). The 4-6-0s, No.5720 Indomitable and, possibly, No.5684 Jutland, are both long firebox types, the former with replacement Fowler tender. If the Shap engine is No.5684, this was the original double chimney 'Jubilee', now with a normal boiler – cf also page 97, top. As far as can be seen, all four engines are in unlined black, No.5720 with the post war number positioning on the cab.

Both trains tell us much about travelling conditions in those difficult times; neither has a dining car, both are predominantly third class and both are massive formations – 14 coaches in the Shap view and no less than 16 at Penrith. The carriages also show how the LMS pressed almost everything into service at this time. They cannot all be identified as to type, but in terms of design, the following details can be spotted:- **Shap train:** Stanier brake composite; three LNWR thirds; Stanier third; five more assorted pre-Staniers, mostly thirds (there might just be another brake composite) and all but one pre-Group (LNWR or MR most likely); four more Stanier thirds, including one brake at the rear. **Penrith train:** GSWR brake third; Stanier open third; LMS (1920s pattern) open third; two LNWR corridor thirds; MR or early LMS brake composite; MR clerestory brake composite; four Stanier thirds; five assorted, mostly third class from all three LMS periods plus at least one pre-Group!

This picture, just south of Carlisle, shows the very end of the 'pure' LMS period on the West Coast route, save for livery and a small modification to the engine. The carriages of the 'up' 'Mid-Day Scot' are all LMS types, the train is still "Lizzie" hauled as of yore and Lady Patricia (now No.46210 and probably blue) is still in charge. Although the engine is still Class 7P (altered by BR to 8P c1951); it now has a domed boiler, probably one of the very first times it was seen in this form.

111

Leeds City was one place where the main line operations of the LMS and LNER came face to face. This is nicely symbolised in this c1950 view at the west end of the station. On the left, Class 5 4-6-0 No.45424 waits to depart with an express whose leading carriage is of LNER origin, while to the right Gresley 'Hunt' Class D49 4-4-0 No.62738 The Zetland also seems impatient to be about its business. There may be no movement here but note how carefully Treacy composed the picture to suggest activity.

(Opposite, above) A common scene at Leeds City was the re-engining of Newcastle-Liverpool expresses from LNER to LMS motive power and vice-versa. This remained purely 'company' in its nature for several years after 1947 and co-incided with Treacy's earlier work in the West Riding. In this view, a pair of 'Jubilees', No.45705 Seahorse and No.45567 South Australia, get under way in 1948 with a train of Gresley coaches, all still carrying LNER varnished teak livery. Both engines have long firebox boilers but No.45567 was one of the original short firebox examples modified to accept the newer type. The train was heading for Manchester and Liverpool and the leading engine is from the former LNWR shed at Leeds, Farnley Junction.

The LNWR route to Liverpool from Leeds was a tough one and double-heading was common. Here is an alternative pairing on a similar working, c1950. This time Manchester based 'Jubilee' No.45595 *Southern Rhodesia* pilots rebuilt Edge Hill 'Patriot' No.45527 *Southport* away from Leeds. The Gresley LNER stock is still varnished teak but the leading Thompson carriage carries BR colours. The last time this picture was published, the train engine was wrongly identified as an Edge Hill 'Royal Scot' – it was an easy mistake to make with the rebuilds.

Treacy rarely ventured onto the Leeds-Manchester main line but when he did, he usually chose an uphill location where engines were working hard. This is Linthwaite between Huddersfield and Marsden at much the same time as the previous view with a third combination of LMS 3-cylinder 4-6-0s on duty. The pilot engine is now a Manchester based unrebuilt 'Patriot' No.45520 Llandudno and this time the train engine **is** a rebuilt 'Scot', possibly No.46109 Royal Engineer. If so, it was based at Leeds. Once again the LNER set of carriages is featured though, in fact, LMS and LNER sets worked turn and turn about until replaced by BR stock.

Approaching Marsden on the Huddersfield-Manchester stretch, a 1947 built Class 5 4-6-0 No.44790 climbs towards Standedge Tunnel with a special working c1950. Not only is all the stock of LMS origin, there is no sign at all – at least in the visible parts of the train – of any first class accommodation. The LMS handled massive special and excursion traffic, for which it often used high capacity open gangwayed stock. Nothing much changed for several years afterwards and apart from the leading brake, all carriages visible are open thirds.

Back to Leeds, this time for the Midland exit towards Shipley, Skipton and Carlisle — familiar Treacy stamping ground. This one has been seen before but savagely cropped; the whole is better than the part! It is a typical LMS scene, albeit just after Nationalisation, with a Bradford train leaving behind the inevitable Compound 4-4-0 No.41080, an early LMS built RH drive example now with Stanier chimney. Although the headlamps say 'express', the carriages are all non-corridor and a fairly untidy assemblage it is: Fowler c1928 composite plus lavatory third brake, followed by a Stanier non-lavatory third brake and third. Only one 'loo' in the whole train and even that one was only third class! It was typical. Other interesting detail includes a classic Midland signal, LMS signal arms on ex-MR posts, a nice collection of vans on the left including a fairly ancient MR or LMS bogie scenery example and a catch point in the foreground which is a fully developed turnout.

By contrast with the previous view and only a year or two later in time, this modern 2-6-4T No.42111, designed by Fairburn in 1945 as a variant of Stanier's 1935 version, is in charge of an equally modern three coach 'Inter-Corridor set', one vehicle still in LMS colours. It is a Low Moor engine and it too is en route from Leeds to Bradford, this time via the ex-LYR route, the location being Holbeck, High Level. This sort of scene is often regarded as being typically late LMS but is in fact, quite phoney, hardware notwithstanding. The engine was not built until 1949 and the two 'Porthole' brake thirds (note the circular toilet windows) did not appear until 1950, both of them in BR red and cream from new — modellers beware!

Back once more to the former Midla[n]
main line North of Leeds where the sight [of]
a Class 4P Compound 4-4-0 piloting [a]
Class 5 4-6-0 occasioned no surpri[se]
whatsoever. The location is Skipton, t[he]
engines are No.41197 and No.44904 a[nd]
the train is a Leeds to Morecambe reside[n]
tial express c1950/1. Everything is pu[re]
LMS and there is added interest in the fa[ct]
that the Compound was shedded at Teb[ay.]
As usual, there is a nice rendition of linesi[de]
and other detail.

More than once I have remarked and tri[ed]
to analyse how the very nature of Treacy[']s
photography allows us to observe t[he]
development of particular aspects of [a]
subject over the years. This was never mo[re]
marked than in his coverage, from 19[46]
onwards of that celebrated LMS and B[R]
train, 'The Thames-Clyde Express'. I ha[ve]
therefore chosen to conclude this chapt[er]
with just some of the views he took durin[g]
the 1946-50 period when the train was pu[re]
LMS. Interestingly, there is not a sing[le]
Settle and Carlisle view among them!

We start (how else?) with the pione[er]
rebuilt 'Royal Scot' and long time Holbe[ck]
resident No.6103 Royal Scots Fusilier [at]
one of Treacy's favourite spots, Marl[ey]
Junction near Keighley – no doubt t[he]
closest bit of railway to his home in th[e]
town! The year is 1946 and the first thr[ee]
carriages repay some close attention. The[y]
are all pre-Stanier and are, respective[ly]
brake first (1927), open first (1927[,]

ntd. from page 116)

lve-wheel first diner (1930). By LMS
ndards this would represent quite a high
portion of 'state apartments' even before
war, much less after! In fact, the open
t is likely to have been downgraded as an
classed' open diner. The rest of the train
s third class Stanier stock.

6103 is on the train again at Skipton
time, possibly only a few weeks or
nths later. There is now an ex-LNWR
brake leading (probably not a regular
urrence) and the 1927 vintage brake
t is still present but the open first has
n replaced by a much newer third class
n carriage – again presumably for
ng. The twelve-wheeler is behind the
er tank but the rest cannot be seen.

rley Junction again, same place, same
le, same engine and same train as
ore, but not the same picture. I guess
is now 1947, for the old brake first has
n replaced by a somewhat newer and
nger example, an 'all steel' carriage of
1 vintage built on the integral construc-
principle without any conventional
derframe trussing. It was probably more
urious too and certainly more modern
king. The rest of the train is as seen in
Skipton view. This is the set also
tured on page 52, lower, in Chapter 3
h the addition of a leading ex-LNWR
brake and hauled by No.6117.

Occasionally, Leeds had no rebuilt 'Sco[t]
for this working, in which case they turne[d]
out a '5XP'. This is Marley Junction aga[in]
from a slightly different angle and t[he]
engine is No.5573 Newfoundland, anoth[er]
famous Holbeck stalwart. The train [is]
unchanged and the period must be la[te]
1947; in 1946, No.5573 was one of only tw[o]
engines painted in an experimental blu[e/]
grey colour by the LMS prior to t[he]
adoption of the 1946 black livery which t[he]
engine is clearly carrying here. Trea[cy]
actually photographed it in both shades a[nd]
also caught the other blue/grey one, 'Duch[-]
ess' 4-6-2 No.6234 Duchess of Aberco[rn]
on the West Coast route!

Holbeck also received some of the first [of]
the rebuilt 'Patriots' and early in 194[8]
No.45530 Sir Frank Ree was on 'Tham[es-]
Clyde' duty leaving Leeds, still with p[re-]
cisely the same set of carriages. The eng[ine]
still carries its LMS colours and there is [a]
welter of period detail to the left of t[he]
picture, not least the suburban carriage. [It]
was originally of the fully panelled type b[ut]
the photograph indicates much lower bo[dy]
panel replacement, not to mention show[ing]
the post war LMS carriage livery with [its]
flat-topped '3s'.

In 1949-50, the 'Thames-Clyde' received another injection of replacement carriages, this time including brand new first class vehicles from the BR built batches of LMS pattern stock which immediately preceded the first BR standard vehicles. This 1950 view, leaving Leeds, shows two of them at the front of the train, a brand new red and cream five compartment brake first and a one year old six compartment full first, still in LMS livery. These gave 66 seats rather than the 27 formerly available in the solitary brake first – the train was clearly getting more popular and something like pre-war conditions were returning. The engine is another of Holbeck's well known 'Scots', No.46117 Welsh Guardsman, still in LMS colours but soon to become BR green and receive smoke deflectors.

This last example of the pretty well undiluted 'LMS' look on the 'Thames-Clyde' also dates from 1950 with Royal Scots Fusilier once again, still in LMS colours but now sporting BR number and new standard BR headboard. The second carriage is still a full first but is now red and cream and this view also allows sight of the new dining provisioning – two open carriages, one each, first and third class, flanking a separate kitchen only car. This had been the pre-war arrangement on this train so things were obviously getting back to normal.

Treacy went on recording this train during the whole of the steam period and well into diesel days and its virtual demise. However, as early as 1951/2, it had already ceased to be a 'proper' LMS train, largely because being one of the more important services, it was also one of the first to receive new BR standard vehicles.

119

We start in a gentle way with 'Royal Scot'
No.6118 Royal Welch Fusilier in full back
gear and held at the shunting signals prior
to running light engine to Edge Hill shed for
servicing. It is a Holyhead engine and had
doubtless arrived a little earlier with a train
from North Wales. The period is c1935-6
and in later years, the platform behind the
tender was to be extended alongside and
beyond the bridge abutments, see page 122.

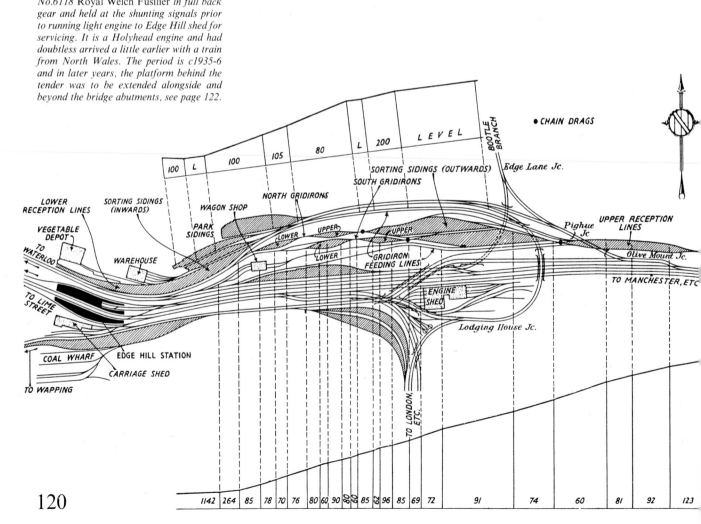

Chapter 6

Lime Street to Wavertree

The close juxtaposition of one not very outstanding terminal station, an exit through a mile or more of deep cavernous cuttings, a through station of no great aesthetic distinction and a complex of railway yards and junctions whose complications and convolutions were such as almost to defy understanding, hardly sounds like a prime recipe for railway or indeed any other sort of pictorialism. Yet it was in this environment that Eric Treacy made some of his most famous and outstanding pictures. It is hardly more than two miles from Liverpool Lime Street Station via Edge Hill to Wavertree Junction and I reckon Treacy knew almost every inch of the way. He returned constantly and almost every picture he took, no matter how similar to the previous one was in some subtle way different. We have seen a few examples already but this section of the book looks at the place in rather more detail. First, however, so as to set the scene and aid orientation, a bit of basic railway history.

The former LNWR terminus at Lime Street was not the first Merseyside 'end point' of Stephenson's pioneering Liverpool and Manchester Railway, but the approaches to it still had to cut through the same rock structures as the original exit from Crown Street (which later became a pure goods depot) and must have been every bit as difficult to construct as the original route from which it diverged at Edge Hill Station. In the opposite direction, the line from Edge Hill struck due East for Manchester but shortly after leaving the station itself, lines diverged both southwards to Crewe and northwards to Bootle. There was also a third converging line from the city side at Edge Hill, the branch which led up from Riverside (for the transatlantic boat traffic) and Waterloo Dock goods station via a long tunnel. There were thus six routes converging at Edge Hill and if to these one then adds a considerable motive power depot and numerous sets of marshalling yards, including the famous Edge Hill 'gridirons', the end product was more than somewhat confusing both geographically and in terms of railway operation. I have, therefore, thought it helpful to append a diagram, not to scale, of the basic track configurations at Edge Hill as they were during LMS ownership in 1938, the very time of Treacy's first exploration of the area. Wavertree and Mossley Hill were, respectively, the first and third stations south of Edge Hill on the Crewe and London line.

Making the business even more interesting was the fact that the whole of this vast complexity of trackage was on a generally rising gradient from West to East. The diagram shows those applicable to the marshalling yards – in which case the gradients could be used beneficially in the gridirons in that they permitted gravity shunting. This advantage did not, however, work in favour of

Diagram of junctions, marshalling and sorting sidings at Edge Hill, LMSR 1938. (Courtesy National Railway Museum)

121

trains coming up from the city direction, whether it be from Wapping Dock via Crown Street, from Lime Street itself or from Waterloo Dock and Riverside. It was rugged going on all three lines and many and splendid were the locomotive pyrotechnics occasioned in overcoming their adverse gradients. Treacy, however, concentrated solely on the main passenger route from Lime Street and this is almost certainly because it was the only one which had any appreciable amount of its gradient in open cutting rather than tunnel – but what a cutting, sheer sided and deep whose innermost recesses hardly ever saw the sunlight. However, when they did, the contrast of light and shade could create the most dramatic effects and there can be no doubt that this is what appealed to Treacy. One can be sure that had he seen any artistic potential in the other two exits, he would have found them! Interestingly too, he never photographed in Lime Street cutting unless the sun was shining.

In point of fact, however, it was the area round Edge Hill itself and the southbound mainline at Wavertree Junction which seems to have claimed most of his time during the later 1930s – and a right royal parade of LMS trains he photographed there during the 1937-9 period. Although he took up residence in Yorkshire in 1945, he never deserted his old Merseyside stamping ground and, indeed, his best work in the cuttings was almost certainly in the 1946-8 period during the changeover from LMS to BR.

In this survey, I have chosen to ignore the time chronology and elected instead to pursue a geographical approach starting at Lime Street Station. As usual, the passage of time has imparted much of historical significance to the Bishop's views of the scene and some of these aspects are, of course, mentioned where thought to be helpful. Essentially, however, this next group of views is mainly a pictorial celebration of one man's territory. He made it his own and few since have dared to try to emulate him, no doubt because they knew they could do no better.

This 1948 view shows a departure from Lime Street taken from almost the directly opposite direction to that of the previous view – note the new platform extension on the left. The engine is Stanier 'Jubilee' No.45704 Leviathan, based at Farnley Junction, Leeds and is undoubtedly setting off for its home city with either a Newcastle or Hull bound train. The coaches are all in LMS colours and the engine livery, such as can be seen, is the short lived experimental LNWR style lined black.

(Opposite, above). The first tunnel out from Lime Street spanned four tracks and was not much more than a long bridge. In this view Edge Hill rebuilt 'Patriot' No.45527 Southport, catches the sunlight as it makes a vigorous start on the hill. The carriages still clearing the platform in the background are at almost the precise position of the engine in the previous view. The date is 1948 but the train cannot be identified, probably for London.

(Opposite, below) Literally a hundred yards further up the bank, another patch of sunshine could be pressed into service(!), this time to illuminate rebuilt 'Royal Scot' No.46138 The London Irish Rifleman on a departing express. This view has been published several times before but always in vertical format and showing the right-hand side only – how much more interesting to see the whole picture. Again the date is 1948 and the engine from Edge Hill.

This group of four views starts with one of Treacy's trainless pictures of the many bridges spanning the four tracks leading up from Lime Street to Edge Hill. Judging by the lack of smoke it is some time since a train passed. Note particularly the nearest bridge. It probably features more than any other in Treacy's views in the cutting and its distinctive mortar courses have framed many a dozen LMS engines as they battle uphill. Two 'Jubilee' pictures have already been seen on page 95; here are three more locomotive types. Note the subtle changes of light and smoke effect and the slightly changed camera position each time, from a near close-up to a long shot framed by the next tunnel mouth. All views date from the 1948-52 period and all three engines were based at Edge Hill. For the record, they are: 'Royal Scot' No.46164 The Artists Rifleman, 'Princess Royal' No.46204 Princess Louise and 'Patriot' No.45533 Lord Rathmore. The two 4-6-0s are in early BR lined black while the 4-6-2 may be either BR blue or newly repainted BR green. The trains are bound for the West of England (note the GWR carriage second behind the 'Royal Scot'), London and the West Riding respectively and the vehicles are in a mixture of liveries.

Out of the last tunnel and into Edge Hill
station – a Liverpool-Newcastle train of
LMS stock heads East for Manchester and
the West Riding behind an aptly named
'Jubilee' No.45708 Resolution, based at
Farnley Junction. The leading carriage is a
composite to a new LMS design, actually
built by BR in 1949-50. They had a slightly
different profile to normal LMS carriages
and were of semi-integral construction,
somewhat akin to the later BR Mark I
stock, but probably more comfortable!

(Opposite) Forward again to another
favourite 'haunt', Edge Hill No.2 Box, just
East of the station platforms and a pair of
Class 5 4-6-0s, Nos 5019 and 5148, based
at Hellifield and Crewe South respectively.
Although carrying express headlamps, both
trains consist of non-corridor stock which in
each case has pre-Group examples leading
(LNWR behind No.5019 and both MR and
LNWR behind No.5148). The upper view
cannot be dated (possibly pre war) but the
lower one must be 1946 or later since the
engine carries the 1946 pattern lettering. It
is a fair bet that the upper view was taken
from a position half way up the signal
ladder visible on the extreme left of the
lower picture and that the latter was
photographed from the verandah of the
signal box itself.

There is a mass of detail in both pictures
which repays careful study, whether it be
the lines bearing right to Waterloo Docks
(above the train engines), the carriages and
wagons parked all over the place or the
complexities of the trackwork itself and the
point rodding. Note too the post war
carriage painting practice of flat topped '3s'
and the placing of a figure '1' on the
carriage window of first class compart-
ments. This is truly a magnificent pair of
'railway' pictures.

(Opposite, above) Just beyond Edge Hill No.2 Box, the first set of lines to bear right linked up with the goods lines from Crown Street but the express trains carried straight on as seen here in the shape of No.6206 Princess Marie Louise making an unconscionable amount of fuss and bother as it gets into its stride with a heavy 'up' express, c1938-9. One guesses that Treacy may have had something to do with the spectacular pyrotechnic display! Once more, peripheral interest abounds whether it be the carriage variety (ex-LNWR brake leading), the goods vans in the sidings or the inscription 'LMS' below the roof of the warehouse.

(Opposite, below) Ten years or so later at the same spot, the signal box has been replaced, the junction to the goods lines relaid with heavier flat bottomed track and the trains are beginning to display a mixture of LMS and BR colours. The train is a local bound for Chester where the engine, Compound No.41121 is based and the formation is a typical LMS mixture; LNWR non-corridor third brake, three LMS non-corridors of two periods (including one Stanier composite and an earlier lavatory third brake) and two late design LMS corridors one of which is a brand new BR built 'Porthole' brake third. The warehouse roof seems to have been re-branded 'LMR'!

This nice high level view of Edge Hill, taken from the road overbridge – see next view – also dates from c1950 and shows a Manchester (Longsight) 'Jubilee' No.45587 Baroda tackling a fourteen coach express unassisted. The last carriage appears to be ex-LNER so it could well be a Newcastle express with a bit of post-BR dilution affecting the otherwise pure LMS formation. This huge train is a far cry from today's pathetic equivalent with no more than seven or eight carriages in charge of more than 2,500hp of Class 47 diesel. Times indeed have changed – as has the railway scene along with them.

This view has been seen before but ne
previously, as far as I am aware, has
whole of the fascinating scene been f
tured. Earlier books have concentra
purely on the two 'Royal Scots', No.6
The Lancer and No.6112 Sherwood Fo
ster. This is a pity for it is a wonder
record of the late 1930s transport en
onment, even to the extent of one of
then very new streamlined Liverpool tra
cars crossing the bridge. Lancer is head
the three coach Liverpool portion of
'Sunny South Express', while the solit
lamp over the left hand buffer of No.611
probably a rear one, the engine being ab
to set back to Lime Street.

In terms of railway 'geography', Ee
Hill No.2 Box is just visible through
arch below the tram while just behind
camera position, the line for Crewe and
South bears away to the right.

A few hundred yards further east from
previous view, the signals give a clear vis.
indication that "Turbomotive", No.6202
just about to bear right for Wavertree a
all points south with the 'up' Merseys
Express'. This engine was something o
'regular' on this working during the la
1930s – as indeed it was when running
BR days for a few weeks as the ill-fa
Princess Anne.

In this view, 'Duchess' Pacific No.6232 Duchess of Montrose leans to the curve between Edge Hill and Wavertree Junction with an 'up' express. This is not the least familiar of Treacy's Liverpool pictures but is rarely shown with the full array of background detail. In the right background can be seen a Stanier 2-6-2T at Edge Hill shed while to the left is an absolutely magnificent array of carriages, vivid confirmation of the fact that the railways in those days were geared up to handle vast numbers of people at short notice. Amongst the types identifiable are both wood panelled and Stanier LMS standard types, quite a few LNWR examples and a solitary GWR 'Toplight' corridor.

A little further round the bend featured in the previous picture, the main line to the south passed below the goods lines which came out of the Edge Hill 'gridirons' via a huge loop – see plan, page 120. Treacy made the bridge where the main line passed beneath the goods lines into something of a trademark. This close-up view shows Compound 4-4-0 No.1166 heading south, c1936, with an intermediate express composed of ex-LNWR and early LMS stock. The smokebox shed plate cannot quite be identified but the engine was probably from the Chester and/or Holyhead area.

A little further south from the bridge and the view was augmented by one of the many tall LNWR signals which were so characteristic of this area in the 1930s. This picture shows blue streamliner No.6224 Princess Alexandra on an 'up' express with at least some coaches for the West of England; the leading vehicle is a GWR brake composite. By this time, c1938, the blue streamliners were beginning to appear on trains other than the 'Coronation Scot' and Treacy recorded several on Merseyside.

The low angle, near head on shot was a very characteristic Treacy 'ploy', rarely better exemplified than in his many studies near Wavertree. Here is a splendid one – 'Royal Scot' No.6155 The Lancer *at almost the same spot as the blue 4-6-2 in the previous view but from a totally different viewpoint. The goods line can be seen behind with a Webb ex-LNWR 0-6-2 'Coal Tank' ambling down the hill towards Wavertree.*

133

Having passed below the goods lines, the passenger trains reached the last part of their virtually uninterrupted climb out of Lime Street and the 'Top of the Hill' was visibly obvious. Treacy loved the place and this is a typical example, 'Princess' 4-6-2 No.6210 Lady Patricia breasting the gradient with at least thirteen bogies in tow and probably more. The train is not identified but the leading carriage is a 1929-30 composite brake, one of the first LMS types to have large side windows. It was clearly functioning as a through coach since the next vehicle, a brake third, forms the first part of the train 'proper'. It could have been from Southport (see page 138 lower) or may even have been the LMS turn to provide a West of England brake composite – see page 132, lower.

Ten years later nothing much seems to have changed, save for the presence of a post war 'Duchess' No.6254 City of Stoke-on-Trent in 1946 livery. The carriages are still a mixture of LMS pre and post 1933 styles but take a closer look at those signals in the left background – the LNWR sentinels have gone, all replaced by LMS standard upper quadrants.

This has to be one of Eric Treacy's finest evocations of the Wavertree scene – a truly memorable impression of 'Royal Scot' No.6157 The Royal Artilleryman *storming up the last few yards of the bank with a Liverpool-West of England express. Little or no detail can be discerned of any of the carriages or other minutiae; this is a classic case of 'never mind the history, just enjoy the view'!*

(Overleaf) For what it is worth, I consider this powerful picture to be Eric Treacy's best ever photograph of his much-visited spot at Wavertree where the goods lines (on the left) came down from the bridge to meet the passenger lines. The twin pairs of LNWR signals frame the main train – as they so often do – but on this occasion he has moved back sufficiently far to get them all in the picture without cropping the tops and has even managed to include the shunting signals on the extreme left. The main train is headed by 'Royal Scot' No.6112 Sherwood Forester. *Not only is it a nigh on perfect picture, 'Treacy's Luck' having also got him a 'Jubilee', No.5708* Resolution *in just the right place as well(!), but it is also a valuable historical record. The 'Jubilee' was based at Farnley Junction (Leeds) and what it and its kind were doing in this location will be explained by the next pair of pictures.*

(Opposite) These two pictures, both familiar Treacy images at Wavertree, have been seen before but never together; yet between them they illustrate a nice little operating 'cameo' which neither does separately. The year is 1938 and Stanier's new non-streamlined 'Duchesses' have just been sent to Camden (London). In the first picture, the last of the series, No.6234 Duchess of Abercorn is heading back for London and waiting on the goods line is another Farnley Junction 'Jubilee', No.5703 Thunderer – see page 136. This route via Lodging House Junction, was one of the ways to get engines 'off-shed' after servicing at Edge Hill – see diagram, page 120 – and was often used for this purpose.

In the next picture, which must have been taken only a few minutes later, Thunderer has gone south to Wavertree Junction and then started to set back to Lime Street on the 'down' main; the LNWR signal by the distant bridge is now 'off' and the 5XP would, in due course, probably be heading back to Manchester and Leeds past the other side of Edge Hill depot with a Hull or Newcastle train. Meantime, as another 'Duchess' Pacific, this time No.6231 Duchess of Atholl sets off for London with a train whose leading vehicle is a through coach from Southport, the 'Jubilee's' place on the goods line has been taken by an unidentified LNWR engine at the head of a through freight, 'waiting for the road' as they say.

Although Treacy favoured Wavertree Station itself far less often than its complex junctions and gradients, this fine view of Class 5XP 'Jubilee' No. 5630 Swaziland passing through the station is an apt way to conclude this survey of Merseyside. The engine was based at Edge Hill and is homeward bound for Liverpool with a 'down' express.

139

Traffic and Trains II
Parcels and Freight

Although the LMS gained probably 60% or more of its revenue from freight and other non-passenger traffic, it has to be admitted that Treacy's pictures did not entirely reflect this situation. In this respect, he was no different from many other photographers and one suspects that there were several good reasons for this, mostly bound up with the nature of railway operation itself. In Treacy's case this imbalance was undoubtedly exaggerated by his well known preference for big express power which in the normal course of events would not be seen on freight workings, but there may have been other reasons too, for there is no evidence that the Bishop deliberately ignored goods and parcels trains should they pass in front of his camera. The fact is that they less often came his way than did the expresses and this again is not surprising.

First and foremost, freight was very much a night time operation as far as the principal routes of the LMS were concerned, whereas 'Treacy's LMS' was very much a day time scene for a variety of reasons. Some of these were based purely on photographic considerations, for he is on record as preferring sunlight to illuminate his views, and moreover, not the weak wintry variety either. In fact he is generally reckoned mostly to have ignored his cameras from November through to March. Secondly, his free time was very constrained and since busy priests do much of their pastoral work when most of us have finished ours, he is unlikely to have been able to get out very much even when the freight began to move on a sunny summer evening, largely because of his church duties. With the exception of holidays, his pictures were taken as opportunity allowed and, in consequence, were mostly taken during the working day.

A third reason was bound up with the nature of the freight traffic itself. Treacy liked to photograph trains at work on the main line (where most of the freight ran at night), so he tended rarely to potter about in the yards where the bulk of the daytime freight activity took place. Railway goods and parcels working had a sort of pattern which by day concentrated in getting the vehicles to the right place to be formed into trains which then set off later in the evening or overnight. The familiar daily 'pick-up' freight was part of this activity and would, of course, be seen by day; it was, however, hardly a main line operation, being much more confined to the branches and secondary routes which Treacy rarely frequented during the LMS period. He therefore missed much of it. Even in our present day, much of the most interesting railway activity takes place when it is too dark for photography by natural light so one need not be surprised that Treacy encountered the same problem.

So much for the reasons why this next section is not quite as

This picture of the now preserved 'Jubilee' No.45593 Kolhapur has been published before, described as a Leeds to Manchester parcels train during the engine's last year of operation 1967. In which case it took a wrong turn some 16 years too soon, for this is Penrith c1951-2 just after the engine received BR green livery – note the tender emblem! Every vehicle in the train is of pre-BR origin and the station is in pure LMS condition, right down to the name-boards. It is, indeed a parcels train and a very typical one too. The leading vehicle is an ex-LNER goods brake and this is followed by an ex-GWR bogie 'Siphon' van and a pair of pre-Group six-wheel Covered Carriage Trucks (ex-LNWR and MR respectively). The rest of the train seems to be composed mostly of perishable cargo vehicles.

(Opposite, above) This early BR view (the faint outline of 'LMS' can just be discerned on the tender of Class 5 4-6-0 No.45494) shows a train of purely freight type vehicles running under 'parcels' headcode and being banked up Shap. Most of the vehicles seem to be ventilated or refrigerated vans but the leading vehicle is a cattle wagon. To run under this code, all vehicles, including the cattle wagon, must have been fully fitted and the fact that the livestock vehicle is in leading position could infer that it was loaded. When loaded cattle wagons were formed up as part of a mixed cargo train, they had to be immediately behind the engine.

extensive as previous chapters, but what can be said is that when Treacy photographed those non-passenger activities which did take place in daylight – and there were more than a few – his record was every bit as detailed and thorough as in his more celebrated express train views. As might be expected, given his preference for main line locations, his coverage tended to be mostly in the field of parcels, express and through freights but this has given us a splendid record of the nature of those workings in LMS days. I have grouped them in descending categories of precedence according to the LMS 1937 rule book and I have thought it helpful to preface each section of this chapter with a brief description of the various classifications, identified, of course, by means of their differing engine headlamp codes.

Parcels Trains

Parcels trains carried two front headlamps, one over the coupling and one over the right hand buffer. In the Rule Book they were defined as 'Parcels, newspaper, fish, meat, fruit, milk, horse or perishable train, composed of coaching stock' and they ranked immediately after passenger carrying trains. Even if vehicles were not exclusively of pure 'coaching stock' type, they had to be 'passenger rated' (ie vacuum brake fitted and, if four-wheelers, of long enough wheelbase for higher speeds), for parcels trains were expected to travel at much the same sort of speeds as passenger trains. Their guaranteed quicker transit commanded a higher rate for cargo so conveyed, and they were often headed by express type locomotives.

(Opposite, below) The 'Horwich Moguls' (railwaymen never used the enthusiasts' term 'Crab') were amongst the least changing engines in visual terms both in LMS and BR days. Generally used for freight work – at which they were regularly the equals of the Stanier Class 5s – the LMS (and BR) trundled them out by the dozen for parcels and empty stock working as well, for they had a good turn of speed. A further reminder of this is shown here in the shape of No.42766 emerging from Gledholt Tunnel, Huddersfield, with a parcels train (incorporating empty stock) heading towards Standedge Tunnel on the former LNWR main line to Manchester. The date is c1956 yet everything is still LMS. One fancies this was just about the end of the undiluted company scene; yet Treacy was there too!

Regular parcels workings used to lea
Leeds City for the Midland Main Line
the Aire Valley and their departures see
regularly to have coincided with Treac
available free time; the shadow directio
suggest a possible lunch break! From t
historical viewpoint, this regular re-visiti
makes this set of four pictures togeth
collectively far more interesting than a
one on its own. My guess is that they
date from c1948-50 and I have arrang
them geographically. They may well sh
the same actual working in each ca
Treacy has left no record, but the dep
allocations of the engines concerned su
gest there may have been two such servic

The first picture shows Leeds bas
LMS standard Compound 4-4-0 No.411
Most of the vehicles are LMS standar
but the leading horsebox could be ex-GW
and the fifth vehicle, a full brake,
ex-GSWR. In the next view, what
probably the same train has another Lee
Compound, this time No.41137 a f
hundred yards further down the line. T
first three vehicles are now four-wheel ve
(including one ex-SR) and the full bra
are of ex-LNER origin.

The third example is in charge of Teb
based ex-MR Class 2P 4-4-0 No.403
seen passing under the high level lines fr
Leeds Central at Holbeck. Again the tr
formation is different. A Southern v
leads, followed by a milk tank, a full bra
and a few more vans. This seems unlikely
have been quite the same working as
first pair of views, but is unquestionably
same service as that shown in the fi
picture, taken a little further down the l
at Holbeck. This shows another Te
based engine, Compound No.41197, wit
very similar formation, including the s
wheel milk tank.

144

Fitted, Express and Through Freight

These three categories represented the bulk of LMS long distance freight movement and Treacy's record seems to have reflected their relative numerical strength in operational terms. In the selection which follows, the preponderance of 'Through' freights is quite noticeable and this merits further explanation.

The 'Fitted' freight (defined as such if at least one third of the vehicles had a continuous brake worked from the engine) was a somewhat rare creature and carried one lamp below the chimney and the second above the right buffer (see page 90, top); its close relative was the not quite so rare 'Express' freight with almost the same headcode (lower lamp above the left buffer). The latter need not have any fully fitted vehicles at all, but if it conveyed at least four so equipped, it could be run under slightly preferential terms as a 'Maltese' freight, a reference to the Maltese Cross symbol by which it was identified in the working

A 'Maltese' freight arrives in Liverpool headed by former LNWR '19in Goods' 4-6-0 No.8815. The train is heading North on the 'down' goods line towards the Edge Hill Gridirons – see diagram, page 120 – and the view is in the opposite direction at this favourite Treacy location, Wavertree Junction, from that shown at, for example page 136. The train is identified as 'Maltese' by the four or five fitted vans at the head.

This next express freight, waiting for a banker at Tebay early in BR days, is probably non-fitted and seems to be composed mostly of sheeted down open merchandise wagons – a very common sight in the steam era. It could, however, be a mineral cargo whose nature needed protection. Not all mineral vehicles ran under 'Mineral' headcode – see page 150. The train engine is Class 8F 2-8-0 No.48660.

This first picture of a train carrying the 'One over One' headcode of a through freight shows somewhat unusual engines for the task, ex-LNWR 'Prince of Wales' 4-6-0 No.25827 piloting 'Jubilee' No.5558 Manitoba out of Liverpool with an 'up' train. Superficially, it looks just like a fitted freight ought to appear but the headcode reveals that none of those vans are likely to have an automatic brake.

timetables. As we have already seen, the LMS got itself out of some of its difficulties by running quite a lot of higher speed freight cargos under 'Parcels' headlamps; even so, by far the commonest long distance category was the 'Through' freight, with the lower headlamp set centrally above the front coupling. About the only condition it had to satisfy was to run at least fifteen miles between stops. It rarely carried fitted vehicles at all and the reason it was so common is no more than a sad commentary on the generally primitive state of most British goods trains during the steam age.

This view, at Cononley in the Aire Valley c1946-7, shows what might be taken for the daily pick-up freight but its headlamps reveal higher status. The engine is, somewhat unusually, an ex-MR Class 2P 4-4-0 No.484 whose 7ft drivers do not seem best suited for this kind of working; it is, however, quite a little train!

(Opposite, above) Class 4F 0-6-0s were the engines which most folk traditionally associated with LMS freight workings, especially on the Midland Division. This example, also at Cononley c1946-7, shows ex-MR Class 4F No.3851 with a southbound through freight, almost certainly one of the many such which ran from Carlisle to Stourton, the home base of the engine. The wagons are almost certainly coal empties which, had they not been running a considerable distance non-stop, could equally well have been operated under empty wagon or mineral headlamps.

(Opposite, below) Skipton based LMS standard Class 4F No.4222 is seen at the same spot at much the same time with what most folk would call a 'Mixed' freight. This particular term had no official status but more than adequately describes the nature of the cargo and vehicles conveyed: covered vans, sheeted down merchandise wagons, cable drums etc.

Almost as common as Class 4Fs during later LMS days and even more so in the BR period were the ubiquitous Class 5 4-6-0s. This is a c1949 view of Upperby based No.45323 in charge of a lengthy and very mixed 'Through' freight heading north up Shap with banking assistance at the rear. Even at this steep angle, the great number and variety of vehicles is apparent and prompts the sad reflection of how much traffic the railways have lost in the years since scenes like this were commonplace. Trains such as this probably generated between one third and one half of total LMS revenue!

Mineral, Empty Wagon and Stopping Freight

A single headlamp over one buffer denoted mineral or empty wagon trains (right buffer) or stopping freights (left buffer) and these were the lowest in the 'pecking order'. This was the realm of the slow moving loose coupled goods train, often with grease rather than oil axleboxes whose ponderously slow progress was the cause of so many of the railway's problems. Expensive goods lines had to be laid to keep them out of the way of faster moving traffic and it is impossible to compute the hundreds of miles of loops, sidings and yards which were needed to accommodate the thousands of wagons which spent relatively little of their time moving compared with standing still! It did of course, have its own fascination and was very much part of the railway scene, but efficient it was not. Treacy made only limited excursions into this field and few at all during the 'pure' LMS period so this section, large though it loomed in reality, is relatively short.

The archetypal mineral working at Ludden-denfoot on the Calder Valley main line of the former LYR was a loaded coal train en route for Lancashire. Such a one is seen here c1950 headed by LMS standard Class 7F 0-8-0 No.49583, based at Newton Heath. It had undoubtedly brought an equally large rake of empties over in the opposite direction at some earlier time.

(Opposite, above) A 'Mineral' train did not necessarily have to convey just mineral wagons and it is hard to tell whether this formation is a mineral train with added vans or an empty wagon train. The engine, a superheated ex-LYR design 0-6-0 No.12619, is working hard so it may be a loaded train. The location is Preston, probably in the late 1930s, and the locomotive carries a former LYR headlamp rather than the LMS standard pattern.

(Opposite, below) Treacy took a number of pictures in the early and mid-1950s which cannot be dated with any precision yet which show no real sign of BR equipment, so slow was the rate of change in the pre-1955 modernisation period. It seems a pity not to use some of them where they genuinely add to the LMS story. This nice close-up shows Class 8F 2-8-0 No.48443 passing over Garsdale Troughs with a southbound stopping freight (probably the daily 'pick-up') and obviously not needing to take any water. It is a nice picture of a long vanished but once everyday scene, although in 'pure' LMS days, the job would far more likely have gone to a Class 3F or 4F 0-6-0.

The Class 7Fs were very much associated with the former LYR system and this example, No.49509 is from Agecroft. It is, however, heading back to Lancashire via the old LNWR main line and was photographed at Linthwaite. The headcode in this case probably denotes empty wagon stock – it was certainly not vacuum fitted, this engine has steam brakes only.

This survey of freight activity is concluded with a fine view at Hampstead Road Bridge, just north of Euston in which, somewhat unusually, Stanier 2-cylinder 2-6-4T No.2567 is seen carrying the 'Mineral/Empty wagon' head code. It is a pretty fair bet that these were empty vans being moved out of the unloading bays and that the engine was on a 'filling-in' turn between outer suburban workings to Tring, Bletchley or even Northampton, for it carries a Watford shed code. The date is c1947.

153

This view of a southbound local passenger train leaving Preston, c1937 is not the least familiar of Treacy's images but I am not repeating it here simply because it is a cracking good picture but largely because its high technical quality reveals the nature of a quite extraordinary train. The fact of the 'Royal Scot' No.6162 Queen's Westminster Rifleman *on a local working makes it a little unusual but the real historical interest lies in the carriages.*

At first glance it can clearly be seen that they are formed into two three coach sets of non-corridors with brakes at each end and, indeed, one can just see part of the first set's 'branding' visible behind the tender. Closer examination reveals that all six carriages are third class only and even closer analysis brings to light the fact that every single vehicle is to a different style viz: LMS standard steel panelled brake third c1930, LMS standard fully wood panelled third c1925, ex-LNWR arc roof brake third

c1900, ex-LNWR low elliptical roof brake third c1905, ex-LNWR elliptical roof full third c1910 and LMS Stanier pattern brake third c1934. This sort of random assemblage was by no means untypical of the LMS, no matter how much the Company might profess its faith in the virtues of standardisation. In fact, a mixed formation of this sort was far more typical than a set of standard carriages, a point amply demonstrated by the rest of the views in this Chapter.

However, if to all this one then adds the features of the still very strong LNWR environment, not to mention the group of platelayers in the left distance, one has yet another well nigh perfect encapsulation of the total LMS synthesis of the 1930s – and just look at that wonderful array of fixed distant signals on the further of the two gantries! Altogether it makes for a most tremendous 'railway' picture.

154

Chapter 8

Traffic and Trains III
Local Passenger

In steam days, the stopping passenger train was usually the sort which most of us tended to use but it has to be conceded that Eric Treacy does not seem to have fallen quite as much under its spell as did many folk. It was, of course, usually a rather low-key and leisurely sort of operation, rarely taxing the efforts of either engine or crew – local trains seldom gave cause for the sort of spectacular smoke and steam effects which Treacy loved so much – and this may have had something to do with it.

From the historical standpoint this is rather a pity, for it was often the local train which produced the longest lasting survivors from previous eras, whether they be locomotives or carriages. Treacy seems not to have been too concerned about this and, in consequence, his local coverage is distinctly patchy. Where it exists at all, it is every bit as good, both technically and artistically, as his more customary images but I have found it rather more difficult to locate anything like the same depth of coverage, hence the relative shortness of this chapter. However, all is not lost, for those pictures which he did take do actually give quite a fair representation of many typical aspects of LMS stopping train operation, even though one could wish he had done more. In consequence and so as to ensure sufficient variety, I have had to stray rather deeper into the BR period to find examples in some cases. Fortunately, they are still pure 'LMS' both in concept and hardware, for nothing of any real significance actually changed until the dmu revolution of the late 1950s and 1960s. Therefore, in order to set the background to this admittedly limited survey, I thought it might be helpful to give a very brief resumé of LMS local passenger operations. They did not die with the Company!

Basically, LMS stopping trains came in two sorts, suburban and 'others'. As far as can be seen, Treacy only photographed the 'others' which in a sense is fortunate, for they were by far the more interesting. Pure suburban trains, whether they be in Birmingham, Glasgow, London, Manchester or elsewhere, usually consisted of fairly tidy sets of standardised carriages hauled by but one or two classes of equally standardised locomotives (precise types of engine and carriage depending, of course, on the specific area in question) but for the most part they did not go un-recorded. Away from these areas, there was a sort of 'anything goes' philosophy whose only common factor was the solitary headlamp below the locomotive chimney; in so far as Treacy bothered with them at all, he seems to have subconsciously appreciated that they were possibly a bit more interesting! In consequence, we do have a revealing, if rather limited picture of some of their more variable manifestations.

What can be said from the outset is that even Treacy's limited coverage bears witness to the fact that there were no 'typical'

LMS stopping trains outside the purely suburban areas. They consisted of any number of carriages between one and a dozen, the carriage types were chosen from anything capable of turning wheels (including the latest corridors) and although the engines were normally drawn from the 'second eleven', there was no prima facie reason why the latest express types should not be used if circumstances so demanded. All told, therefore, it was quite a fascinating business and the following few pages try to show some of it.

In this view, it is the train itself which commands attention. The location is yet again Wavertree Junction c1937, this time right at the place where the goods lines diverge from the main line to Lime Street. The service itself is probably a Crewe Liverpool working and is headed by ex-LNWR 'George the Fifth' class 4-4-0 No.25376 Snipe. The train is another typically LMS 'mixed bag'. The leading vehicle is a former M&GSWR corridor third, probably added as a strengthener while the rest of the carriages are non-corridors. An ex-LNWR low elliptical brake third leads followed by a couple of LMS standards of different periods, one being a composite and there would be another brake third out of sight. Perceptive students of carriage history would have made a bee-line for the first vehicle, regardless of the fact that it was nearly forty years old!

Here at Euxton Junction c1983, former LYR 4-6-0 No.10412 has charge of a really quite superior quality local, but then, the engine was based at Blackpool so I guess that was where the train had started. Behind the fish van (from Fleetwood?) comes an almost brand new 'Two Coach Set No.226' (one can actually read its number) composed of Stanier brake third plus composite. Next is a three coach gangwayed set of pre-Stanier LMS standard stock: brake composite c1927, open third and corridor third brake, both c1930

156

is local train at Standish, near Wigan,
tures an almost brand new 'Jubilee'
.5718 Dreadnought (note the 1936
tern insignia) on what was probably no
re than a three coach ex-LNWR set
sisting of two brake thirds plus a
nposite. The latter, the central of the
ee vehicles and built c1920, was newer
n the brake ends which were of the low
ptical roof type, c1905. It was a common
WR and LMS practice to put a newer
nposite between older third brakes. It
only saved the cost of a complete new
of coaches but also ensured that the first
ss passengers rode in a newer vehicle!
re Treacy has recorded a good example.
e train also retains the fully lined livery,
icating a no later than 1933 repaint.

eacy's visits to North Wales usually
centrated on the principal expresses at
ces like Holyhead but here he has
orded the somewhat unusual instance of
former LNWR 0-8-0, No.49291 on
ssenger excursion working at Penrhyn
ings, c1948 – note the new BR number in
46 style LMS characters. The train is
tincly 'modern' essentially a four coach
nier corridor formation (two brake
rds, one third and one composite) with a
engthening non-corridor third 'cut in'
ead of the last brake.

Turning attention now to the Midland Division of the LMS just after the war, we start with a typical four coach formation near Skipton behind ex-MR Class 2P 4-4-0 No.359. Again – see page 157, top – it is a three coach ex-LNWR set with a newer elliptical roof composite inserted between two low roof brake thirds, this time strengthened in the rear by a fully panelled LMS standard full third of c1925-8 vintage. For some reason, ex-LNWR non-corridors were quite commonplace on this part of the former MR during the final LMS days.

Heading north near Gargrave, this double headed six-coach local has the equivalent of Class 8 power – Compound 4-4-0 No.1006 (an ex-MR example) and LMS built Class 4F 0-6-0 No.4296. All six vehicles are corridors and the first three form a set, two brake thirds plus composite. This time, however, the composite is some ten years older than the brake ends! The three rear vehicles, less distinct than usual in a Treacy picture, are two Staniers and an unidentified brake, probably of earlier vintage. The date is c1946 but Treacy does not identify the working. It was probably Morecambe bound with the 4F added to save a light engine working – Compounds normally had this sort of task to themselves.

This is an almost identical job to that of the last view but now in the opposite direction at Marley Junction behind LMS built Compound No.1081. Treacy did identify this view as a Morecambe-Leeds train but called it an express – probably because of the nature of the train itself, quite lengthy and entirely corridor. This sort of formation, although running under stopping headlamps, was quite characteristic of the 'outer residential' trains of the time, the LMS no doubt feeling that it would better retain its wealthier commuters if it gave them decent carriages! This was the time, of course, when Morecambe was almost 'Leeds/Bradford by the Sea'. The angle of view is too steep to determine the precise formation but it is clearly a mixture of Stanier and older stock.

The Compound 4-4-0s had almost their last fling down the Aire Valley during late LMS and early BR days and anything other than the main line expresses was likely to get one from time to time. This train is a somewhat mysterious local leaving Leeds City c1951 behind a very scruffy No.41096 based at Nottingham. It could have been bound for Sheffield and points south or Leeds may have commandeered it for a Bradford turn – it's anyone's guess. Behind the six-wheel van are two LMS non-corridors and a corridor third brake, all from the pre-1930 period.

159

In pre-dmu days, which in the West Ridi... began in 1955, many of the LMS loc... passenger services in the Leeds area we... handled by two coach sets and a 2-6-2... Nothing had changed when this picture w... taken of Manningham based Stan... 2-6-2T No. 40112, just past Holbeck L... Level with a little train probably bound ... Ilkley or Otley. The pairing of the no... corridor carriages is typical 'random LM... – Stanier non-lavatory composite plus 19... vintage lavatory third class brake.

Leeds City served many local destinati... on the LMS and the old style of operat... lasted well into BR days. This c1951 v... shows a Huddersfield bound departu... headed by Fowler Class 4P 2-6-... No.42412, one of the final series with ... doors. The three vehicles visible, all seem... gly still in degraded LMS livery, ... ex-LYR, LMS standard and ex-LN... respectively – a by no means uncharact... istic mixture – see page 161 lower.

That the pure LMS scene lasted well into BR days is well shown in this delightfully sp view of a three coach local at ringwood Junction, Huddersfield, behind other Huddersfield based 2-6-4T .42384, this time one of the earlier riety with open sided cab. Only the later R tank side emblem and the 55G shed-ate reveal it to be late 1950s for the track still bullhead and the carriages are two -LNWR (brake third plus composite) d one early LMS standard (lavatory rd class brake).

e Calder Valley main line was ex-LYR rritory and there were still plenty of propriate reminders even in early BR ys. This typical example shows a werby Bridge ex-LYR 2-4-2T No.50777 charge of a three coach set consisting of -LNWR brake third, LMS standard mposite, ex-LYR brake third. Note, yet ain, the slightly newer composite sandwi-ed between two older brakes.

These two pictures of a Webb desi[gn]
ex-LNWR 2-4-2T No.46701, taken ea[rly]
in BR days at Bangor, show something [of]
the way Treacy often approached eng[ine]
portraiture. In the first picture he puts [the]
locomotive in close juxtaposition not on[ly]
with the sort of machine which eventua[lly]
replaced it, Class 2 2-6-2T No. 41230 bu[ilt]
by BR to Ivatt's 1946 design, but also w[ith]
another highly characteristic LMS pr[o]
duct, Class 5 4-6-0 No.44911. There is a[lso]
sufficient of the shed visible to make [it]
something more than a mere record of [an]
engine; it is in fact almost a pot[ted]
summary of more than 50 years of locom[o]
tive evolution from LNWR to BR.

The second view is, of course, a qui[te]
excellent close-up detail shot of the bunk[er]
top and cab, but by including some of [the]
background as well as framing it betwe[en]
two LMS upper quadrant shunting signa[ls]
what could have been a routine record sh[ot]
becomes much more of a picture.

Chapter 9

Locomotive Portraits

It is said that one of the entries in 'Who's Who' concerning Bishop Treacy quoted as one of his hobbies: 'pottering about in engine sheds'. This was undoubtedly true and, indeed, locomotive depots were some of the few areas of the railway, other than the lineside itself, where Treacy spent any appreciable amount of time. He certainly does not seem to have haunted the goods yards or carriage sidings to anything like the extent to which he gave favour to the engine sheds. The steam locomotive was his first love so not surprisingly, the majority of Treacy's static shots seem to feature it and he gave us some fine 'portrait' studies. He also recorded typical shed activity and, on more than a few occasions, took formal locomotive pictures at other locations. It is this side of the LMS which is featured here.

As always, one gets the feeling that Treacy was seeking for a picture as well as a record and although there were many dozens of photographers who probably recorded far more formal views of many more different class types than did Treacy, there was usually something distinctive about his efforts – if no more than the positioning of the camera to get the best effect. Treacy was not too concerned with capturing every possible class but those he did manage to record were almost always displayed to best advantage. There was quite regularly something else of interest in the picture as well, for although he did from time to time fill the viewfinder with but one solitary image, he more usually seems to have preferred a 'grouping' of engines, some human interest or a bit of the essential background so as to add more atmosphere to the picture.

In this selection, I have tried to choose examples of all these various approaches and, as usual, the passage of time since most of them were taken has made some of the then peripheral detail of even more historic interest. There is no particular theme to the particular locomotive types featured save that I have arranged them broadly in chronological locomotive design order (ie pre-Group first and Ivatt LMS types last) rather than put them in the date order they were taken. In this context, they span the period from the 1930s to early BR and I have tried to ensure that no view shows any post-LMS modifications, save for locomotive livery.

Treacy did not, if truth be told, fall as much under the spell of the old pre-Group engines as did many of his contemporaries, but when he did take a 'straight' engine picture without even the vestige of background detail, he often preferred the older ones as this delightful pair of former LNWR 4-4-0s bear witness. In technical terms the pictures cannot be faulted; the tonal range is superb and for this reason they give a great deal of very clear information about the LMS changes to two famous engine classes.

No.25272 Brindley, at Wavertree is a Chester based superheated 'Precursor' with original pattern round top boiler and separate splashers while No.25321 Lord Loch is a belpaire boilered 'George the Fifth' at its home base, Edge Hill. When introduced, the 'Georges' were a superheated development of the 'Precursors' and had single splashers. Later, many 'Precursors' were given superheaters and became, in effect, 'Georges' in all but name. The belpaire boiler came in during LMS days and both types could be seen on either class, as could the modified cab roof profile also shown here. This was a modification to clear the LMS composite loading gauge. Both engines are in lined black livery with LMS duplicate series numbers and even the tenders are different, that behind No.25321 being of a slightly older design than the one fitted to No.25272.

Perhaps one of Treacy's reasons for frequenting Edge Hill so often was that engines came there from all over the place for servicing and/or turning. This is a saturated boiler ex-LYR Aspinall 0-6-0 now based at Shrewsbury. Once again the image is nice and crisp, allowing much detail to be seen, even on a plain black engine. The 0-6-0s were one of several really long-lived ex-LYR types, whether saturated or superheated, largely because they were well designed and substantially built. A superheated example may be seen on page 151, top.

Here is another typical Treacy 'grouping', again spanning the years – see page 162, top. The location is now Holbeck (Leeds) in 1948 and lined up are a pre-Group ex-LYR radial 2-4-2T No.50630 dating from late Victorian times, an unidentified Midland designed but LMS built Class 4F 0-6-0 from the 1920s and an almost brand new rebuilt 'Royal Scot' 4-6-0 No.46117 Welsh Guardsman. The tank engine was based at Manningham for use, inter alia, on the Bradford-Leeds local trains on the ex-Midland line.

The Aspinall 2-4-Ts were another excellent ex-LYR type and the transfer of some of them to the former Midland lines was an interesting 'role-reversal' of normal LMS practice (ie MR engines inflicted on everybody!). These are two further Manningham based examples and as was often the case, Treacy put both of them into an appropriate environmental setting, with considerable added interest in this case, bearing in mind their former surroundings.

The engines themselves represent the saturated belpaire boiler variant just before and after Nationalisation. No.10899,

photographed at Hellifield, c1947 was actually built new by Hughes, who introduced a distinctive extended smokebox and bunker with the characteristic belpaire firebox. note the retention of Ramsbottom safety valves. No.50686, at Leeds City c1951, was a belpaire rebuild of a short bunker Aspinall engine, again with extended smokebox. Other extended boiler belpaire engines from this class were, of course, superheated and could be distinguished by the more forward position of the chimney.

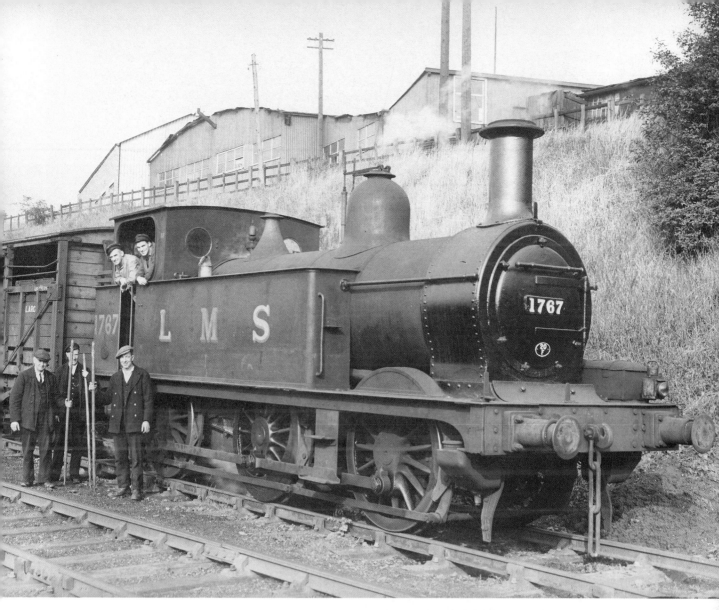

This delightful view of ex-MR Johnson Class 1F 0-6-0T No.1767, c1947, is one of Bishop Treacy's rare excursions into the more bucolic part of the railway. The location is Skipton and the engine, based there, is carrying stopping freight headlamps. One suspects that this was a deliberately posed shot before the morning pick-up freight got under way – possibly to the Grassington Branch? Yet again, Treacy has added railway interest to a fine record of the engine itself.

Another c1947 view, this time on the four-track section of the Midland Main Line between Keighley and Bingley, shows a Skipton based Midland built Class 4F No.3904 passing a through freight headed by a Holbeck Class 8F No.8176. Although essentially a locomotive picture, this too is of greater interest because of its surroundings. The 0-6-0 is carrying a 'pick-up freight' headlamp (rather than the 'light engine/engine plus brake van(s)' code over the centre coupling) so it is clearly off on its way to collect some 'trade'. What is mildly surprising is that a more important train should be side-tracked to let it pass.

168

Quite late in its life, the LMS built a new 'Roundhouse' pattern shed at Carlisle (Upperby) and Treacy spent much time there. This is a lovely grouping of both locomotives and environment. The shed itself, starkly new in concrete, forms an interesting contrast with the older LNWR building on the left, while the engines themselves are a typical mixture of LMS types, from left to right: an unidentified 'Patriot' Class 5XP 4-6-0, LMS standard Class 2P 4-4-0 No.652 and Class 5 4-6-0s Nos 5299 and 5139. Note, incidentally the different pattern front numberplates on this pair, reflecting the years when built, 1937 and 1935 respectively. Deep in the shadows on the right, one of the two original 'Patriots', No.5501 St Dunstans can just be distinguished. It was renamed from Sir Frank Ree in 1937.

These two views, separated by only a few years, span the LMS/BR transition period and were taken at Leeds City c1947 and Dumfries c1951. No.521 is a 7ft driving wheel RH drive ex-MR Class 2P 4-4-0 with an exhaust steam injector and LMS type boiler mountings. It is seen in final LMS plain black livery and both carriages to the left display the 1946-7 style of flat topped '3s' on the doors. No.40688 is an LMS built LH drive 6ft 9in version of the same type in the first BR mixed traffic livery, introduced in 1948 before the adoption of the Lion and Wheel tender emblem. Again, the background environment adds to the scene and in the case of No.40688 serves as a reminder that these 4-4-0s were very much part of the former GSWR scene for many years. The engine itself was based at Hurlford during the brief time in the early 1950s when it carried shed code 30B.

This interesting pair of pictures again contains rather more of interest than simply the engines themselves. In the first view, taken at Shap Summit c1938, two banking engines, both members of the final series of Fowler Class 4P 2-6-4Ts. Nos 2404 and 2424 (note the cab doors and side windows) are seen waiting to return to Tebay after assisting trains up the hill. The use of big passenger tanks for this particular purpose on Shap Bank was of very long standing, from LNWR through to BR days, and remained a feature at Tebay until the end of steam. The 5ft 9in wheels of the LMS 2-6-4Ts were ideally suited to a task which could involve anything between a principal express and a long freight train.

The second early BR period view at Manchester London Road shows two more members of the same class but from the earlier series with 'open sided' cabs, about to become involved in much more typical duties for the class – local passenger working. No.42391 was based locally at Longsight, but No.42365 was from Buxton, which no doubt was its next destination.

The 'Princess' Pacifics were the most famous of Stanier's earlier designs. The main batch was built in 1935 and this view shows the last of them. No.46212 Duchess of Kent climbing Shap in 1948. The engine is still in pure LMS condition, the angle of view clearly revealing the proportions of the ten ton tenders which replaced the earlier nine ton variety in 1936-7. It also carries experimental BR black livery and Treacy has again included just sufficient of the background to make even this simple view into something more than a mere record.

One of the earliest of Stanier's designs was the Class 5XP 'Jubilee' type which first appeared in 1934. In preservation they have become even better known, particularly No.5690 Leander. This fine semi-formal view shows it at Shildon during the 1975 Stockton & Darlington celebrations. The beautiful finish – if truth be told probably even better than the LMS achieved(!) – makes it clear why it was generally regarded as the best turned out locomotive at that particular event. The picture is, of course, not strictly LMS at all, but the clarity of detail from an unusual angle makes it well worth including.

Stanier's new designs emerged quite quickly over a period of five years between 1933 and 1938. In 1935, one of the best looking, albeit probably the feeblest of his efforts was the Class 3P 2-6-2T. The design was not a total failure and many were built, but they did not entirely displace the earlier pre-Group designs, a point well illustrated in this 1948 view at Llandudno Junction shed with No.40209 alongside an unidentified Aspinall ex-LYR 2-4-2T. It was not until the advent of the later Ivatt 2-6-2Ts – see page 175, lower – that the final inroads were made into pre-1923 types.

The 2-8-0 Class 8F freight engines were introduced in 1935. They were built over a ten year period, becoming the largest of all the Stanier classes numerically and had a complex history, many serving overseas and others being built by the GWR, LNER and SR during the Second World War. This view shows an immaculate LMS built No.8329 at Holbeck c1946/7, carrying its running number in the post war position on the cabside. It was rare for these engines to be so clean at this time and it is likely the engine was recently ex-shops. No.8329 was shedded at Heaton Mersey and was built at Crewe in 1944.

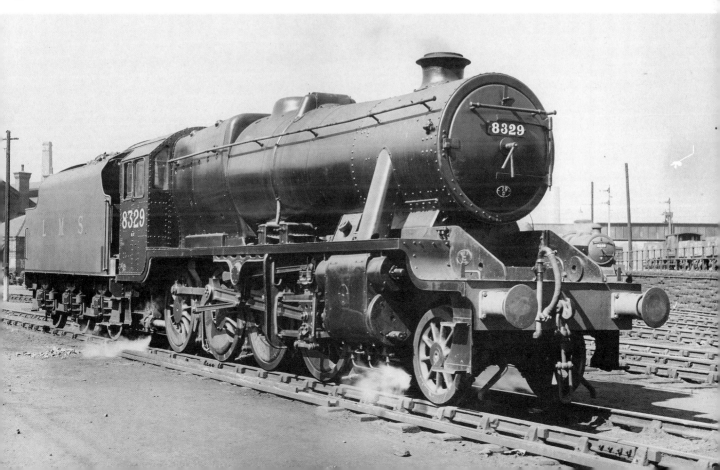

This formal view of the then brand new streamlined Stanier 4-6-2 No.6229 Duchess of Hamilton at Edge Hill in 1939 is a record shot but with a unique difference. The engine is actually painted works grey and is seen running in prior to being returned to Crewe works for a full repaint in crimson and gold. After that it will exchange identity with No.6220 Coronation and go off to the New York World's Fair masquerading as the latter locomotive. It was destined to be 1942 before the engine came back to Britain and resumed its real identity. One wonders how much of this information was known to Treacy, or anyone else for that matter, when he took the picture – my guess is that he was simply intrigued by the unexpected sight of a drab grey streamliner. This engine is, of course, now preserved in BR condition at the National Railway Museum.

By contrast with the previous view, this picture shows the final LMS form of most of the former streamliners. No.6223 Princess Alice is seen here in 1947 at Carlisle adding a van to a northbound express and is painted in the full version of the LMS 1946 livery. By the end of the LMS period, only two of these engines remained streamlined and one of them, by strange coincidence happened to be Duchess of Hamilton.

The last independent days of the LMS saw first Fairburn and later Ivatt in charge of locomotive affairs and, although not strictly responsible for their design (it was pure Stanier in fact), it was they, particularly Ivatt, who organised and implemented the bulk of the rebuilding of the 'Royal Scot' class to the taper boiler form from 1943 onwards. Here is a nice classic Treacy view of one of the first so treated, No.46146 The Rifle Brigade at its home base, Holyhead in 1948 with two Class 5 4-6-0s in attendance, Nos 45402 (from Mold Junction) and 45249.

Although Ivatt did not become CME of the LMS until 1945, his short-lived predecessor in that office. Fairburn, was more of an electrical than a mechanical engineer so Ivatt tended to have most of the responsibility for steam development after about 1943. Most of his work was a development of that of Stanier but he did introduce three new designs, all of them an embodiment of the 'ease of maintenance' philosophy developed during the Stanier years. Perhaps the best of them were the Class 2 engines, tank and tender. This is Class 2 2-6-2T No.41247 built in 1949 and seen about a year later at Derby. Apart from the engine livery, all else is still pure LMS and although the train could just be an express working, the apparent express headlamps could equally well have been one each, red and white, thus revealing a locomotive on station pilot duty.

Chapter 10

The Total Railway Scene

I have said earlier in these pages that Treacy's pictures are not easily categorised. This is partly because most of them work at a multiplicity of levels and partly because they were not really taken with a view to being analysed in the way I have attempted. Indeed, it may even seem presumptuous to try to read so much into images which were, above all, taken as much to express feelings as facts, however much interest the latter may possess. It therefore seemed most appropriate that this review should conclude with a somewhat random series of pictures, linked only by the fact that the total scene seemed rather more important than any one aspect of it. Above all things, it was the totality of the railway which most interested Treacy and it is this which was at the heart of his work.

I have therefore chosen another mixed bag with which to end this book. Some of them are quite well known, others not. In some cases they stand alone and in other cases they work best when seen as one of a series but in all cases they add something to our knowledge of the total railway environment of nearly half a century ago. Although I have arranged them in approximate date order and continued to try to analyse some of the more interesting points revealed, especially in the background, they are above all mainly chosen to indicate the general nature of Treacy's work on the LMS and give pleasure to the reader.

In the last analysis it has to be conceded that Treacy's view of the LMS was not the most definitive portrayal of the Company, for it was devoid of many of those aspects of the railway which would be needed for a totally balanced view. Moreover, his was a railway where the sun mostly shone and the sky was usually blue! But given these limitations and regardless of whether one looks for technical quality, artistry or historical interest, 'Eric Treacy's LMS', as revealed by his pictures, was not only a very interesting bit of our heritage but was also a totally pleasurable visual experience. Bishop Treacy enjoyed his 'railway pottering' and relished the pleasure his pictures gave to others. He was also a man of great joy, a sentiment I have tried to keep in mind as I assembled this selection. If even some of this feeling has come through in these pages I shall be well pleased.

We start this last selection with another of Treacy's Edge Hill views, this time 'Royal Scot' No.6127 Old Contemptibles, a Camden locomotive heading back to London a few hundred yards out from Edge Hill No.2 Box, faintly visible under the left hand arch of the road bridge. This is one of his earlier views, c1936, the 'Royal Scot' not yet having received its curved top smoke deflectors. Technically it is not the best image either, there being some loss of definition on the left (the part usually cropped when this picture has been used before!). Yet it is a true railway 'picture' and there is much of historic interest too, whether it be the LNWR signals, the variation of carriage types or the pre-1937 liveries of the goods wagons to the right, one of which is an ex-LNWR brake van.

Shap Summit itself was one of the less frequented of Treacy's locations in the fell country but in this apparently conventional 1937 view, he has recorded much of interest. The engine heading south is the unique 'Princess' 4-6-2 No.6205 with derived inside valve gear, Princess Victoria and the train, the 'up' 'Mid-Day Scot', consists of a mixture of all three LMS design periods, the first being an early 1926 'all-steel' full brake still in full livery. For a few years, the LMS pursued a policy which often put this type of carriage at the head of many principal expresses, believing its construction to offer more protection in case of accident. To the left in the 'down' loop, completing the typical LMS mixture of periods, is a set of turn of the century ex-LNWR six-wheelers forming a workmen's train.

The earliest days of 'Treacy's LMS' pretty well co-incided with Stanier's major re-stocking of the locomotive fleet. By far the most common of the new types was the Class 5 4-6-0 and Treacy's record quickly revealed the great variety of duties which these versatile machines could tackle. This and the next picture are typical. As usual, not only are they superb and vivid evocations of the scene, but they also contain a multiplicity of once familiar detail which the passage of some fifty years has rendered historic.

This first view, taken at Preston in 1936, shows one of the first Armstrong Whitworth batch of domeless engines, No.5199, departing south with a through freight, almost certainly for the Midland Division. The engine is based at Nottingham and the leading brake van is either a late Midland or early LMS example built to Midland design. The engine is still quite new and the red lining can clearly be distinguished. The LNWR signal gantries nicely complete the mixture.

Messrs Armstrong Whitworth were given the contract to build all the Class 5s numbered between 5125 and 5451 during 1935-7 and with No.5225, the domed series began. This lovely view at Penryn sidings, probably taken in 1938, shows one of the 1937 series, No.5346 based locally at Bangor, in charge of an 'up' local composed of former LNWR corridor stock, save for the Stanier brake just discernible as the last vehicle. The fact that the angle of view is almost the same as the previous picture enables the subtle visual differences between these first two series of Class 5s to be compared – even down to the rivet arrangements on smokebox and footplate!

The engine is also carrying visible signs of the short-lived 1936 livery experiment with sans serif characters, including front numberplate.

This, in itself, would be sufficient to make this picture a valuable record but when to it is also added the LMS replacement upper quadrant arms on the old LNWR signal posts, the signal box itself and the wholly agreeable composition of the entire picture (not forgetting the fireman leaning out as bonus!) then one has the encapsulation of the total railway environment which Treacy made peculiarly his own.

This group of four pictures, all taken at Edge Hill No.2 Box, are, of course, linked both by location and locomotive type (unrebuilt 'Patriot' Class 5XP) and some of them may be familiar to readers. They could well have come earlier in this survey on an individual basis but I have put them here because, when taken together, they seem to say so much more, not least because the first three of them all show the same Edge Hill 'Patriot' locomotive, No.5527 Southport, engaged in a variety of different duties during 1937-8.

No.5527 received its name in 1937 and the first view of it, piloted by ex-MR Class 2P 4-4-0 No.471 must have been taken soon afterwards; No.471 is in the 1936 livery, a style already obsolete when Southport was named. The train is obviously headed for Crewe and points south and the 4-4-0 may

simply be on pilot duty to get it back to home base. This engine pairing gives a vivid reminder of how Midland locomotive lineaments took over the LMS in pre-Stanier days, whether it be in the form of new standard types or simply by transfer of genuine MR engines to former LNWR sheds. Note too the vans behind the 'Patriot'. The leading example is a six-wheel (MR or LMS) fish or meat van, the second vehicle being one of the somewhat rare ex-LNWR bullion vans.

The second and third views show the engine unassisted with two quite differently styled trains – note the ex-LYR brake composite leading in one case. It is difficult to date either with precision but they are probably a year or two later than the double headed example, the evidence being given by the wagons in the background. All three

pictures are interesting in this respect, not least in terms of the number and variety of freight vehicles to be seen. However, whereas the company wagons in the first view mostly still carry large identification letters, those in the second and third pictures show an increased proportion with smaller lettering in the left hand lower corner, an idea first introduced only in 1936.

Finally, the last picture, showing No.5520 Llandudno, is a post war record of the same scene. The engine is still red (just) but the flat topped '3s' on the carriage sides, the changes in wagon livery and the presence of two LMS post war 'plywood' vans, all reveal a date some ten years after the previous pictures. What is, perhaps most interesting is how little things had changed at the fundamental level.

Every picture tells a story, so they say, *but sometimes two can give even more infor- mation as this pair of c1947 views reveal. In the first picture, a stopping passenger train is held at the termination of the 'down' 'slow' line at Marley Junction in order to let a main line express overtake and in the second shot, the local is just departing past the bracket signal indicating that it must re-join the main line. The taller of these two 'splitting' arms, still at danger, controlled the continuation of the 'down' 'slow' line, from this point it carried on to Thwaites Junction as a goods only line. Note too that these bracket signals are of LMS upper quadrant style whereas the main line is still controlled by a genuine ex-MR signal.*

So far so good, but what about the two engine combinations? The express, formed of Stanier stock, is headed by an ex-MR Class 4F 0-6-0 No.3944 piloting an un- dentified ex-MR Class 3P 'Belpaire' 4-4-0 while the slow train, composed of ex-MR low roof suburban stock is in charge of a Fowler belpaire boilered rebuild of ex-MR Johnson Class 2F 0-6-0 No.3078 piloting a Class 5 4-6-0 No.5392. There was in truth a rather delightful 'anything goes' character- istic to much LMS working at this time and Treacy has caught it perfectly in these pictures.

The introduction by the LMS of Britain's first main line diesel locomotive, No.10000, in December 1947 caused great interest, especially when, in 1948, it was joined by its 'twin' No.10001. They were painted glossy black with aluminium trim and, for a year or two, they were put in double harness to work the 'Royal Scot' train turn and turn about with Stanier 4-6-2s. Only No.10000 received 'LMS' lettering but for several years they both ran in their original livery. In these views, they are first seen at Preston on one of the first occasions they ran as a pair (the train is still in LMS livery) while the second view shows them leaving Carlisle c1949-50 with the 'Royal Scot' train newly repainted in BR red and cream. Treacy regarded diesels as a poor substitute for steam in photographic terms, but at least he did record them from the outset.

These splendid panoramic views of Carlisle Upperby, see also pages 9 and 168, provide a clear record of the changing scene at the transition between the LMS and BR. The first picture, taken late in 1947, shows a wholly LMS state of affairs dominated by the Stanier breed, in particular the Class 5 4-6-0s which account for some 50% of the dozen or so engines in view. Not all can be identified but to the right of rebuilt 'Royal Scot' No.6128 The Lovat Scouts are Nos 5323, 5258 and 4786 respectively, the latter almost brand new in post war style lettering. To the left of the 'Scot' is a solitary 'Jubilee', probably No.5728 Defiance.

In the second view, taken in the early 1950s, the camera position has moved closer to the shed itself and reveals an almost totally different array of locomotives, albeit still wholly LMS in origin. There is now only one Stanier type in evidence, Class 8F 2-8-0 No.48512, the rest being either early LMS standard designs (Class 3F 0-6-0Ts including No.47614 and Class 2P 4-4-0s Nos 40582 and 40628) or unidentified ex-LNWR 0-8-0s. It may, perhaps, be presumed that the two pictures were taken at different times of the day but Treacy gives no information at all on this or any other aspect of these fascinating pictures.

Continuing with the transition theme between LMS and BR, this attractively composed view shows experimentally blue painted 4-6-2 No.46227 Duchess of Devonshire *climbing Shap in 1948 with a train still painted 'LMS'. The picture is not unknown but it was not until preparing this book that I realised it also included another typical bit of the Shap scene in the form of a descending banking engine in the left distance.*

This transitional view at Lancaster, c1950, shows rather more BR carriage livery but there is still some LMS red visible in the typically mixed set of LMS coaches forming a southbound express headed by Class 5 4-6-0 No. 45299. The Class 4F No.4032 on local freight duty is still in LMS livery while the 'Patriot' entering the picture on the right is No.45537 Private E. Sykes V.C., *fairly newly repainted in BR green.*

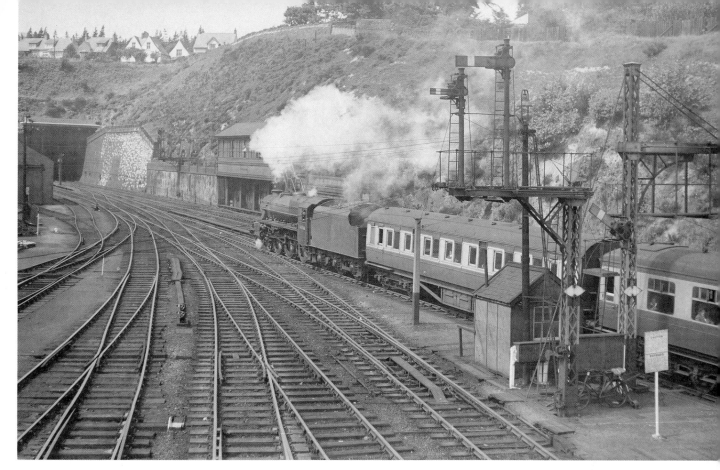

These two similarly composed views at the 'down' end of Bangor station are further examples of the changeover period. They are, typically, undated in Treacy's record but cannot, in my estimation, be much later than 1950-51. The second carriage in the upper picture still carries GWR livery and the typical ex-LNWR bilingual 'Caution' boards still seem to be painted in LMS style as do the signal posts. The train engine is Class 5 No.44766 and the leading carriage is a c1927 built open third of the wooden panelled type.

The second picture is again characteristically pre-BR in terms of 'hardware'. Although the two unidentified Stanier 2-6-4Ts, Stanier 2-6-2T No.40132 and rebuilt 'Royal Scot' No.46139 The Welch Regiment all carry their correct new BR liveries, the mixed rake of carriages in the background reveals both GWR and LMS colours as well as the new BR style. It was in fact quite customary for locomotives to receive their new identity quite a bit sooner than the rolling stock since they tended to be repainted rather more frequently.

1950, Carlisle Kingmoor shed became
A (it reverted to 12A later) so 'Jubilee'
0.45657 *Tyrwhitt* cannot have been pass-
g through Dumfries any earlier than that
ar, but neither can it have been too much
er. Everything is still LMS save for the
t bottomed track. The Class 2P in the
reground has yet to receive its BR lined
ack livery so all points to a fairly early
te. The main train cannot be identified
could, perhaps, be the afternoon
rking to Leeds; there is a twelve-wheel
ning car in the formation. In the
ckground, the ex-Caledonian locomotive
es serve as reminders that much former
SWR territory was operated by engines
the 'auld enemy' after the early slaughter
the ex-GSWR locomotive fleet.

pposite) This view at Kyle of Lochalsh
a truly timeless quality to it. A former
aledonian Railway 0-4-4T shunts the yard
d one doubts if the station 'furniture' had
anged in a generation. The picture cannot
dated (probably the early 1950s) but the
gle of view is such that one cannot even
stinguish the BR livery on the engine and
e whole scene itself is entirely typical of
s remote LMS outpost during Company
ys.

r quite a time after Nationalisation, the
rmer LMS lines retained the Company
le of train identification prefaced by the
ial letter of the appropriate LMS
erating division. This is Central Division
ex-LYR area) train No.C234 heading
st through Sowerby Bridge behind Class
No.44823 whose home base was Agecroft.
e ultimate destination is not recorded but
e train may have been bound for one of
e coastal resorts in either Lancashire or
rth Wales.

The visual indication of the Ivatt regime was rather more familiar after Nationalisation than before, but the concept and hardware was totally LMS, nowhere better exemplified than the use to which his Class 2 2-6-2Ts were put. These engines were designed to offer a thoroughly modern alternative to the former custom of using superannuated relics of the pre-Group era on secondary workings and in this example, No.41217 (based at Barrow) is on just such duty, a push-pull train consisting of a solitary Stanier third class carriage at the Coniston Lake terminus of the former Furness Railway branch line from Foxfield. Only ten of these useful little engines had been built by the end of the LMS period but they became very common after 1947, the class eventually totalling 130 engines, not to mention the almost identical BR version which followed them. No.41217 was one of the first BR batch to the LMS design, built at Crewe in 1948.

(Opposite, below) In this scene, Ivatt 2-6-2T No.41239 is in charge of a stopping passenger train running into Bangor c1950. The engine is the newest feature in this view for the train is the usual heterogeneous LMS mish-mash of types. They are, however, all gangwayed; a former LNWR corridor third leads (still in LMS colours), followed by a Stanier third brake and a 1926 vintage 'all-steel' open third. Amongst the other interesting features may be noted the LNWR bracket signals, the LMS upper quadrant signal by the tunnel mouth, the white painted buffer stops (no doubt painted thus because of the dark background of the high retaining wall) and the three-way turnout trailing to the 'down' main line. This latter feature would almost certainly not find favour in the present day.

The first of Ivatt's larger Class 4 2-6-0 tender engines only just managed to beat the LMS/BR deadline and only the first three actually carried LMS colours. Interestingly too, only Horwich of the former LMS works actually built any, many of the BR built examples coming from former LNER works at Doncaster and Darlington. Although eventually totalling some 162 units, the 'pure' LMS styling was confined to the first 50 which originally had double chimneys as shown here on Horwich built No.43034, dating from 1949. The visual lines of this final LMS design did not meet with universal approval, moreover the double chimneys were both technically and visually disastrous! The chimneys were eventually replaced with a single exhaust but the visual lines, of course, more than accurately predicted those of the soon to be introduced BR Standard types.

The engine featured here was based at Tebay and is seen leaving Leeds City c1950 with a most curious carriage formation carrying express headlamps. The red and cream carriages are all LMS gangwayed third class types, two side corridor brakes and two 56 seat opens, while the fourth carriage appears to be an ex-MR non-corridor third. The train may well have been an excursion since this class of engine was really conceived as a modern replacement for the ubiquitous Class 4F 0-6-0 and was usually used on freight. Note too the upper quadrant arms on the ex-MR signal posts and the teak liveried LNER pattern third class carriage on the left. It was one of the former Cheshire Lines fleet and why it was at Leeds is anyone's guess.

191

"Evening at Camden MPD" is the only clue given to the details of this fine evocative view. It is likely to have been taken in the early 1950s but is a wholly pre-BR scene. The engines are 'bedded down' for the night and an air of peace and tranquility prevails with just a few wisps of smoke to catch the evening sunlight and give the right amount of life to the scene. As ever, the picture is beautifully composed and entirely characteristic of the Railway Bishop's view of the railway. As such, it seems a highly appropriate note on which to take leave of 'Eric Treacy's LMS'.

THE END